Dedicated to the martyrs of Gaza, all victims of Zionist-imperialist barbarism, and the memory of those killed in the fight against it

This special issue is titled 'For Palestine'. The semantic choice here is deliberate. An earlier incarnation of the title was 'On Palestine' but, while working on the issue, the thought occurred to me that too often work on Palestine, notably in academia, is written from up high, simply on the topic. Content to hide behind spurious notions of impartiality and academic objectivity, a clear position against Zionist settler colonialism – and the suffering, displacement and oppression that is inherent to it – is never taken. Likewise, the Palestinians' fundamental legal and moral right to armed resistance against their oppressors is rarely, if ever, endorsed.

The intent of this issue and its contributions, therefore, is not merely to analyse, write or speak on the Palestinian cause in a detached capacity but rather to speak in solidarity with it. This does not mean to lower the standards and intellectual rigour of our work, but rather to make clear that it springs from a position that is resolutely in opposition to Israel and its continued occupation of Palestine and the slaughter, imprisonment, and torture of its people.

Though the exact direction in which things develop from this juncture remains unclear, it is already evident that the events of October 7th and the devastating destruction inflicted by Israel in the following weeks have made a return to the previous status quo impossible – cementing the closure of one historical epoch and the opening of another. Palestine was always a political litmus test, as the common refrain goes, but as Abdaljawad Omar remarks in this issue, recent events have starkly demonstrated the extent to which the Palestinian cause 'reveals hidden discourses of imperialisms and forces centres of power to reveal their schizophrenic stances and hypocritical posturing'. In several Western countries, notably the US, UK and Germany, the liberal mask and associated niceties have been jettisoned fully in the service of full-blooded support for Israel's genocidal war – to the extent that even calling for a cease-fire has itself been equated with genocide. For Max Ajl, writing in these pages, the logic behind these actions – which are not without risk to Western governments – 'is the logic of monopoly attempting to defend itself and the consciousness which bodyguards it with fire from the sky… And it is a logic which might yet meet its end in that crossroads of continents, that salient, and city and their camps and their people'.

The extent to which US imperialism will wage war to defend its settler colonial proxy remains an open question, and one which is of central importance to the world. Indeed, in his contribution to this issue, Bikrum Gill makes a compelling case that, from this point onwards, the victory of the Palestinian war of national liberation is now inevitable. A consistent theme throughout several contributions is the contention that the military balance has inalterably shifted against Israel, especially given the role of Hizbullah and the broader Axis of Resistance – an issue expounded upon at length in the interview with Amal Saad.

In that spirit, it is our hope that this issue will educate, inspire, and perhaps even provoke those who are only in abstract solidarity with the cause – finding themselves moving away from it the moment the Palestinians cease to be virtuous victims and fight their oppressors. The same applies to those who do not see Israel's central function within the US imperialist system, and who instead place too much emphasis on the so-called Israel Lobby as their lens through which to understand events.

As Suleiman Hodali's contribution to this issue teaches us, the fifth Executive Committee for Afro-Asian Peoples' Solidarity was held in Gaza in December 1961. It articulated the 'menace' posed by Israel beyond the scope of its colonial regime in Palestine by affirming that:

> Israel is an aggressive entity propped up by imperialism to be used in striking and menacing national liberation movements in the Middle East area, infiltrating to the other parts of Asia and Africa and that Israel is a tool in the hand of neo-colonialism, as proved by events and therefore the Committee draws the attention of all Afro-Asian peoples to the reality of this colonialist tool and its danger to World Peace.

Over 60 years later, the Committee's words ring true.

Israel is a clear threat to world peace, and every decent human being should stand in opposition to it not only on the basis of the moral necessity of supporting the colonised Palestinian people but because the Zionist state – and its sponsors – represent a direct threat to our collective security and safety. We should be under no illusions: what they are able to get away with imposing on Gaza today, will be imposed elsewhere tomorrow upon the next group of people considered disposable and marked for extermination.

– Louis Allday

Misreading Palestine

Max Ajl

The recent period has seen the bloom of two falsehoods, stemming from the same root of irrationality, glibly ahistorical narratives, and disinterest in understanding struggles for national liberation against imperialism. One: Benjamin Netanyahu more-or-less conspired with Hamas to maintain the Palestinian national division and empowered the movement in Gaza. Two: Israel and its parasitic lobby drive America into irrational warmongering.

'The Lobby' made us do it is nothing new. It has been a cheap lie sold by the Gulf ruling classes to cover up their profitable integration into the US defence-financial umbrella, by counterintelligence funded antisemites sent to destroy the Palestine movement, by Nazis, by the US strategic professoriate like John Mearsheimer worrying about American decline, and recently in the *New Left Review*'s warning that support for Israel 'has historically exceeded any reasonable political calculus'. (When did Marxists decide it is their job to whisper to the exterminationist class that their calculus is off?)[1]

The 'Netanyahu courted Hamas' fairytale is newer, an odd chimaera of the older truth that Israel and the US preferred Hamas – but, seldom mentioned, also Fatah – to Marxist-led Palestinian forces in the 1980s, and the newer truth that Netanyahu made deals that had allowed Hamas some financial manoeuvring space since 2014. We may later consider the origins of each trope. For now, let us consider their content.

Israel, pound for pound, is the best investment the US has ever made. Israel is the purest expression of Western power, combining militarism, imperialism, settler colonialism, counterinsurgency, occupation, racism, instilling ideological defeat, huge profitable war-making and hi-tech development into a manticore of destruction, death, and mayhem. From Israel's victory in the 1948-1949 war, US planners saw the country as a regional military power that could contain Arab military and political ambitions.[2] Amidst France's imperial sunset in the Arab region, the country aligned with Israel – trying to deliver a blow to Nasserist Egypt through the 1956 Tripartite Aggression with Britain and Israel, and armouring Zionism for its successful 1967 war against radical Arab nationalism in the frontline states. Green-lit by the US, the war left the Syrian Ba'athist fusion of Arab nationalism and Marxist-Leninism in shambles and slammed the Nasserist national development project. Israel also became a useful assassin, eliminating Arab radical luminaries from Mehdi Ben Barka to Ghassan Kanafani.

From 1970 onwards, US military aid into Israel turned the country into a unique asset: an offshore arms factory; a regional irritant to Arab peace, stability, and popular regional development; a destructive gyro of worldwide counterinsurgency; a black hole drawing in regional surpluses and devoting them to endless defensive and offensive armament, away from social-popular welfare spending and non-military development. Uniquely, the US allowed Israel to keep the military aid partially within the country, slowly and steadily building up a massive military industrial capacity.[3] Meanwhile, US-based capital inflows accelerated, taking advantage of Israel's highly educated workforce in the defence sector, resting upon super-exploiting the Palestinian colonial underclass in other sectors. In return, Israel armed reactionary forces world-wide:[4] from Argentina to Brazil to Chile, helping evade Congressional restrictions on arms shipments to the Nicaraguan Contras[5] and advanced armaments to the South African apartheid regime.[6] On a world scale, Israel has protected the political architecture of global capitalism. And its US domestic adjunct, the Anti-Defamation League, presaged wider Zionist capitalist investment in repression by carrying out wide-ranging spying on anti-racist, anti-Zionist, Arab-American and anti-apartheid movements.[7]

Throughout this period, the US-Israeli 'Special Relationship' grew ever-more-intimate as relentless imperial proxy warfare and sanctions – from Libya[8] to Lebanon[9] – tarnished developmentalism, degraded republican aspirations, and often evaporated regional Marxism. Class inequalities widened as the Gulf, Egypt, and Lebanon became nodes of regional and global accumulation. The Israeli option for boosting world-wide accumulation through wars on republicanism and revolution served the US ruling class well.

The 'peace process,' known as Oslo, imposed after the fall of the USSR and the encirclement of Ba'athist Iraq, sought neo-colonial neoliberalism under military occupation in the West Bank and the Gaza Strip as part of the post-Soviet attempt to crystallise 'the end of history' through neutralising or evaporating remaining sources of friction or strategic obstacles to the US project. Incoming Palestinian diaspora capital alongside a corrupt Palestinian Authority (PA) was the US's junior partner in the state-building agenda. Israeli capital became a seamless transnational component of the US's globalisation project, with large elements in burgeoning hi-tech counterinsurgency.

Oslo was a legal vector for the growth of the political asphyxiation mechanisms of the so-called terror lists, as the US moved to post-Soviet mop-up operations. The rejectionist forces – those carrying the lion's share of the current resistance operations, namely Hamas and Islamic Jihad, alongside the Popular Front for the Liberation of Palestine – were placed on terror lists, joined by remaining armed communist insurgencies in the Philippines and Colombia, and practically the state of Iran in its entirety through the listing of the Iranian Revolutionary Guards Corps. Palestinian parties faced the death of a thousand cuts as they haemorrhaged cadre to the NGOs erected by the aid industry. Palestinian development deteriorated into an apolitical process of governance, growth, and isolated project work.

Although throughout this period the US ruling class's coffers swelled and Israel became ever more central to global counterinsurgency, wall-building, surveillance, and policing, the US operation failed to close the Palestinian file. Armed resistance, anti-corruption, and a web of civil society welfare institutions gave Hamas the legitimacy to win the 2006 Palestinian elections.[10] Although soon the external political wing would be wooed by the US's most sophisticated proxy, Qatar, the military wing in the Gaza Strip remained close with its Iranian, Lebanese, and Syrian allies. Meanwhile, the IDF's failure against Hezbollah in Lebanon in 2006 set the stage for the redirection:[11]

arming, training, funding, and through the Gulf media, ideological inculcation of sectarian Sunni proxy militias meant to shatter Arab popular consensus around resistance and, since 2011, to set them loose towards the end of regional de-development and state collapse.[12]

Those lines of division emerged openly with the 2011 US proxy war on Syria,[13] the defection of Hamas' political leadership from Damascus to Qatar, and the US aim to gut the armed regional asymmetric resistance movements, while sanctioning and making open warfare, whether through proxy arming of the Free Syrian Army or other militia, or directly, on their state sponsors and logistical backbones – Iran and Syria.

12 years of regional warfare, 100,000s of Arabs dead, Yemeni and Syrian cities bombarded and burnt out, and four wars in the Gaza Strip – 2008/9, 2012, 2014, 2021 – led up to the October 7 attacks. Within the Gaza Strip itself, the resistance made the case to the population that they were a political externality to Saudi/Israeli/US rapprochement and normalisation. That no one was going to do anything for Gaza unless they did something for themselves. That the siege was filling every horizon.

The 'Netanyahu enabled Hamas' distortion rests on the correct statement that Netanyahu dealt indirectly with Hamas via Qatar and allowed the formation of a permit regime for Palestinian Gaza guest workers. This was meant to ensure relative quiet in the South. Far from Hamas collaborating with Netanyahu, or policing the ceasefire, this set-up was an achievement of the Palestinian resistance, allowing it the appearance of political stillness on its surface waters while underneath it moved fast and built up a deep defensive infrastructure. The lie is meant to suggest that Hamas' strength is due to conspiracy with Israel, when Hamas simply expresses the nationalist aspirations of the Palestinian people.

This tall tale has also suggested that Netanyahu wished to avoid direct talks with the PA in Ramallah towards a peace agreement. The lie is the implication that the neo-colonial PA is a force for state building and Palestinian sovereignty. In fact, it is the velvet – more often these days, mailed – gauntlet of neo-colonial collaboration in the West Bank, amidst PA coordination with Israel and the murder of anti-collaborationist cadre like Nizar Banat in 2021. It is also legible only against the background of Qatar's creeping normalisation with Israel and its regional agenda of a sophisticated defanging of the resistance project.

This brings us to October 7, and to examining what has developed in the popular cradle of the Gaza Strip and in the surrounding societies. Within each of them, there are growing anti-systemic or pro-sovereign militia and republican armies arrayed from Lebanon to Iraq, Yemen to Iran. As Al-Amjad Salama notes, 'one of the fundamental factors we observe when examining the resistance forces across the region is the popular embrace … a form of resource mobilisation,' adding that 'one of the most crucial aspects of mobilisation for the forces in the resistance axis is the mobilisation of material resources,' especially human beings.[14]

What is this force, these human beings, referred to in this word – resistance?

First, literally, we refer to the achievement of the poorest and most strategically disadvantaged people on the planet. Within the encircled and immiserated Gaza Strip, many of the Al-Qassam fighters are orphans. Amidst closure and de-development, the popular resistance has been able to consolidate an arsenal and bring 1.5% of its population into a guerrilla force of 30,000-40,000 men that can – man for man – outmatch nearly any in the world.

The resistance, secondly, has alloyed ideological commitment, willingness to sacrifice for their people, and technological ingenuity into armed capacity capable of going head-to-head with a nuclear power from underground tunnels, the 'rear base' and physical strategic depth needed for guerilla insurgency. The concrete is their mountains. From there they have imperilled an enemy with orders of magnitude higher GDP per capita – Israeli GDP is at $52,000 a year, with arsenals worth billions.

Third, the resistance, in launching its October 7 operation, is an example to the world that post-Soviet asphyxiation and extermination procedures, sanctions and terror lists and aid-based countermeasures, could not prevent the rise of a disciplined and new national movement from raising its head to the sky.

Fourth, the popular cradle brings the word resistance beyond armed men to doctors going to their deaths in lieu of abandoning their patients and women and men in the Gaza Strip's North – facing white phosphorus rather than abandoning their homes. It is precisely the strength of the civilian commitment to the national project that provokes US-Israeli extermination:[15] 'the "civilian" officials, including hospital administrators and school administrators, and also the entire Gaza population' are, as a result, the targets – not out of cruelty but to break Hamas by breaking its cradle.

Fifth, through these achievements, the Palestinian resistance has been able to present an acute threat to the settler-capitalist property structures called Israel, to militarised accumulation, to the world's workshop for counterinsurgency technology, and to the entire architecture of regional repression with its associated petrodollar flows, treasury and security purchases, and arms merchandising. For capitalism is not just the smooth clockwork of accumulation through generalised commodity exchange and labour exploitation, it is the machinery of violence – its technology – which ensures the smooth running of the clock, the thingification of its human elements, the political decisions to maintain and rework the machinery of monopoly accumulation, and the waste of human lives which is increasingly the core Arab input into global capitalism.

More worryingly from the perspective of monopoly power, the Palestinian resistance is not alone. It is part of a regional populist resistance enfolding the poorest people on Earth. Yemeni GDP per capita is $677, and its 200,000 men under arms have ground to dust US/Gulf Cooperation Council mercenary armies in large portions of Yemen. They bear an explicitly anti-US and anti-Israel ideology, a considerable arsenal, substantial battlefield experience and a banner of revolutionary republicanism reminiscent of the Golden Age of Arab nationalism. Syria, at unimaginable cost, has isolated US proxy forces numbering in the hundreds of thousands at their apex, maintained state functions, and preserved logistical and material corridors for the resistance. 100,000, at least, are under arms in Hizbullah, now an elite hybrid fighting force substantially more advanced and experienced than it was in 2006.

It is unimaginable that the neocolonial authoritarian states nor their US benefactor would remotely tolerate massive working-class militia which speak a language of justice and republicanism and raise arms against those states' sponsors. In turn, it is as natural as the sun rising in the East that the US, the UK, Germany, France, and their Gulf and Arab satraps would converge on support for Israel as the spear's tip of the assault on the surrounding Arab popular militia.

And because Israel is the keystone of the regional imperialist order – maintained not by hegemonic consensus but the brutality of Apaches and Merkavas – it is as natural as water falling from clouds that what has developed in the Gaza Strip, as soon as it mobilised politically and militarily, would incite the Western reaction to wipe it from the face of the Earth and impose unimaginable horror to terrify the Palestinian, Arab, and Third World people to never again raise their heads.

The October 7 operation has perhaps overcome the central role of the Israeli state in accumulation on a world scale: ingraining a state of defeat amongst the Arab working classes, as part-and-parcel of the post-Soviet ideological defeat imposed by capital upon labour globally. Deterrence is the form that defeat takes when pushed to the military plane, and Israel openly admits that its deterrence has been shattered.

Seen from this perspective, the risks run by the western capitalist states – their imposition of fascist regulation against freedoms of speech and assembly, their backing for genocide, their desperation to see the Palestinian armed militia wiped from the face of the Earth – is logical, reasonable, and rational in its sociopathy. It is the logic of monopoly attempting to defend itself and the consciousness which bodyguards it with fire from the sky. It is a logic which fills graveyards, and a logic which makes orphans, and it is a logic which might yet meet its end in that crossroads of continents – that salient, and city and their camps and their people.

Max Ajl is a senior fellow in the Department of Conflict and Development Studies at Ghent University and an editor at Agrarian South. He is the author of A People's Green New Deal. His writings on Arab development can be found on ResearchGate.

References

1   Oliver Eagelton, "Imperial Designs", *New Left Review*, November 3 2023.
2   Irene Gendzier, "U.S. Policy in Israel/Palestine, 1948: The Forgotten History", *Middle East Policy*, 18:1, Spring 2011.
3   Larry Lockwood, "Israel's Expanding Arms Industry", *Journal of Palestine Studies*, 1:4, Summer 1972.
4   Benjamin Beit-Hallahmi, *The Israeli Connection: Who Israel Arms and Why* (Pantheon Books, 1987).
5   Margo Gutierrez, Milton Jamail, 'Israel in Central America', *MERIP*, 140, May/June 1986.
6   Aluf Benn, 'How South Africa's Apartheid Regime Saved Israel's Defence Industry', *Haaretz*, December 10 2013.
7   'The Business of Backlash: The Attack on the Palestinian Movement and Other Movements for Social Justice', *IJAN*, March 2015.
8   Matteo Capasso, 'War, Waste, And the Destruction of Libya', *Security in Context*, December 27 2022.
9   Nathaniel George, 'A Third World War: Revolution, Counterrevolution, and Empire in Lebanon, 1967–1977', Diss. Rice University, 2019.
10   Sara Roy, *Hamas and Civil Society in Gaza: Engaging the Islamist Social Sector*, (Princeton University Press, 2014).
11   Seymour Hersh, 'The Redirection', *The New Yorker*, February 25 2007.
12   Ali Kadri, *Arab Development Denied: Dynamics of Accumulation by Wars of Encroachment* (Anthem Press, 2015).
13   Patrick Higgins, 'Gunning for Damascus: The US War on the Syrian Arab Republic', *Middle East Critique*, 32:2, 2023.
14   Al-Amjad Salama, 'An Bidayat al-Kalam fi Mahdar al-Muwajahat al-Kubra', *al-Akhbar*, 18 October 2023.
15   Jonathan Ofir, 'Influential Israeli national security leader makes the case for genocide in Gaza', *Mondoweiss*, November 20 2023.

An Interview with Abdaljawad Omar on October 7th and the Palestinian Resistance

Louis Allday: Thank you so much for agreeing to do this interview, Abdaljawad. I was blown away by your recent article in *Mondoweiss*, 'Hopeful pathologies in the war for Palestine: a reply to Adam Shatz', so I am very happy to be speaking to you.

Your article, as the title says, is a response to Adam Shatz's article 'Vengeful Pathologies' that was published in the *London Review of Books*, but it's actually about so much more than that and is honestly the best thing that I've read so far about October 7th. Could you explain your motivations in responding to Shatz's piece and why you thought it was important to do so?

Abdeljawad Omar: In Adam Schatz's piece, the element I find unforgivable is not his moral aversion to Palestinian violence – nor his condemnation of Palestinian resistance, nor even his adoption of what can only be described as a highly curated Israeli narrative shaped through military censorship and misinformation/disinformation to project a specific image of events in the Gaza envelope. The most critical issue is his reductionist view of resistance itself, equating it to 'primordial instincts' and unchecked passions while dismissing any other possibilities. Although I did not mention this in my critique, this is the revealing aspect – not necessarily of Shatz himself, but of an entire liberal analytical stream. This perspective not only morally dismisses resistance, as Judith Butler does, for instance, but also overlooks its political potential. Unlike Butler's essay on the compass of mourning, Shatz at least attempts to delve into the political and military logic and possibilities. However, he ultimately dismisses them with dystopian, dark undertones, portraying the widespread increase of fascism as an inevitable outcome. He only offers us the nightmare. I think when thinkers offer only nightmares, they are consciously or unconsciously invested in the status-quo. They offer us the monsters so we remain committed to existing structures, to hinge our political wager on sustaining a reality, even if this reality means, as Ghassan Kanafani explicated, that Palestinians live in a world that is not theirs. For Shatz, the nightmare is on the horizon but for us Palestinians we live in the nightmare and have for at least 75 years.

This is a political sin par excellence, because if anything Palestinian resistance operates on a highly tangled architecture of emotions and passions – chief among them to employ its potencies and whatever meagre power to widen the horizon of political possibilities – to crack history open and yes, the nightmare is a possibility and yes, Palestinian resistance is imperfect, but the nightmare is not the only thing one on offer. For some of our so-called allies to foreclose those possibilities is to me 'unforgivable'. I am less interested in aversions to violence or even to moral condemnations of Palestinian actions, and resistance like any other institution should be criticised. I remain however adamant, as history will show, that what happened in the Gaza envelope is profoundly different to how it was presented. Again this does not mean that Palestinian fighters did not kill any civilians, but the image presented to us is incomplete at best and a more complicated narrative will emerge when the battle subsides.

What this informs us, or tells us, is that many thinkers are capable of a stance that at its heart is anti-intellectual, and to me rejecting thinking is what you expect from fascists, not leftist or progressive allies. Zizek is another example; he speaks of Palestinian actions and resistance as a sign of Palestinian deprivation and desperateness. Indeed, accomplished philosophers and writers all of a sudden become reductionists and ideologues. When Palestinians are desperate [and] they do not turn to resistance, instead they become what Mahmoud Abbas has become – collaborators in their own slow but steady unmaking and erasure. Resistance is and always was a hopeful pathology, even if it ultimately fails to snatch a victory.

LA: Your words remind me of Mahdi Amel's famous maxim, 'you're not defeated so long as you're resisting'. Related to that and what you have just described regarding anti-intellectual reactions to Palestinian resistance, something that was very striking to me in the aftermath of October 7th was how few people – even those ostensibly supportive of the Palestinian cause – were either unwilling or unable to consider what the strategic aims and intentions behind launching such an operation actually were. Many people portrayed it simplistically, as some kind of inevitable or spontaneous explosion of anger and violence brought about by the long-term siege of Gaza and the suffering it inflicts. In your article you make clear why this is such a misleading and patronising position to adopt, notably as the Israeli narrative of

events has collapsed so dramatically. Could you briefly explain your argument here?

AO: There is a rich genealogy and history of resistance, a consistent thread that has been largely ignored by both Western intellectuals and many Palestinians. Palestinian universities do not offer academic programs in resistance studies, this is a significant omission. Even detailed academic analyses, like those of Yezid Sayigh, which accurately depict the decline of the Palestinian revolution, are not exhaustive and at times are unsympathetic to the ability of Palestinians to dent the international system. The trope of the profane Palestinian fighter remains a figure misunderstood on their own terms, and it remains an orientalist trope. It celebrates, for instance, figures like Mahmoud Abbas for his collaboration and torture of Palestinians and even provides such figures with political and moral legitimacy, but places the Palestinian fighter outside the realm of comprehension or intellectual engagement. The space for Palestinians to articulate their struggle is confined within legal constructs and liberal narratives of victimhood, which offer only a superficial treatment of agency, civil resistance, and nonviolence, ignoring the harsh realities Palestinians face and the conditions that breed Palestinian liberation organisations. Paradoxically, and perhaps disgracefully, it is often scholar-soldiers, those most immersed in comprehending the Palestinian fighter and their military logic, who seek to understand this resistance only to undermine and defeat it.

Regarding the events in the Gaza envelope, the Palestinian military strategy was to target military and security installations with ambitions of taking over settlements and penetrating deeply into the territory. This guerrilla tactic aimed not just to thwart Israeli efforts to retake land but also to hold areas for negotiation, complicating and impeding an easy Israeli counterattack. This approach implicitly reveals that the Israeli counteroffensive was conducted with little regard for Israeli lives.

It is important here to note that Palestinian resistance operates as a 'weaker' force that is generally invested in finding cracks at opportune moments, to snatch an opening. With 2,000-3,000 fighters involved, and both sides taken by surprise by the offensive, much confusion occurs for those doing the penetration and those defending it. It stands to reason that if the outright intention had been to indiscriminately kill, the number of Israeli casualties in the initial days would probably have been significantly higher. The number of forces, the replenishment of these forces and their relative dominion over entire areas suggests as much. Thousands of fighters with hours in civilian space would have simply caused larger casualties.

The other aspect to consider is how deeply militarism is ingrained in Israeli society, evidenced by the widespread possession and knowledge of weaponry use. Observations from Israeli Twitter in the early days revealed journalists and residents discussing how they repelled and killed Palestinian fighters – not military or police, but civilians. This suggests that the confrontations involved not just the Israeli military and special units, but also civilian-soldiers and military-trained police officers. Again, these are only small parts of the larger picture but it remains important because Israel used and employed moral injury to declare its genocidal intent in the open against the Palestinians in Gaza.

LA: It is already plain to see to any informed observer that Israel has suffered a tremendous blow as a result of Operation al-Aqsa Flood, given the centrality of the military to its identity and the sense of security that it is supposed to provide to the population in a settler colony such as Israel. In your opinion, is this a psychological blow that Israel can recover from and what are its broader implications? Especially in light of the losses the Israeli military is currently suffering, both in Gaza and in the north due to attacks

by Hizbullah that are growing in intensity and scope.

AO: Zionist supremacy has been shaped by a paranoiac view of the world, coupled with a military doctrine that revolves around the concept of an Iron Wall as articulated by one of Zionism's founding fathers, Ze'ev Jabotinsky. Israelis are known for their 'existential anxiety' – a profound fear concerning the survival of the 'Jewish state.' Examination of their think tanks, newspapers, and military journals reveals an obsession with perceived threats: the growth of the Palestinian population, Palestinian resistance, the potential of an Iranian nuclear program, and even the capabilities of Arab militaries. Israel is perpetually vigilant, scanning the globe for any conceivable threat whether immediate or distant, hypothetical, or real.

However, paradoxically, this constant vigilance and the drive to transform the unknown into the known, to feel that everything is under control through a paranoiac lens – combined with advanced surveillance technologies, intelligence, cyber capabilities, AI, and both offensive and defensive military strategies – led Israel to believe in the invincibility of its Iron Wall. This belief was a pitfall. On the 7th of October, Israel's perceived security was challenged; the nation had convinced itself of its safety, despite regularly articulating threats and acknowledging vulnerabilities. This public discussion of vulnerability paradoxically engendered a false sense of invincibility, further bolstered by recent Arab normalisation efforts.

Thus, the events of the 7th of October shattered this illusion of invulnerability. There is a stark difference between holding a threat or vulnerability as an abstract possibility and confronting it in reality as a traumatic actuality. Almost instantly, vulnerability shifted from a potential risk to a devastating reality – a 'shattering experience.' It was as if a 'God' suddenly realised their mortality or, in other words, a god discovered they were, after all, human. This is why in that moment we saw the transformation of Israel's liberal and even supposedly leftist streams into fascist undertones. Ben Gvir emerged as a collective Israeli voice, with very small exceptions.

To me, the extent and depth of this experience depends on the current battle in Gaza, West Bank, and Lebanon. It hinges on the ability of Israel to fail in its offensive, denying Israelis an ability to stitch together a narrative of triumph after a drastic failure. But no matter the results of the ongoing campaign, the extent of trust and confidence in Israel's security and military apparatus has been undermined.

Israel's immediate response evokes the spectre of the Nakba and ethnic cleansing, along with the real possibility of driving Gazans to Sinai, before attempting the same with Palestinians in the West Bank. This should tell us that if Israel finds enough international willingness to turn a blind eye it will attempt to commit in this century another Nakba.

LA: The barbaric violence that Israel has unleashed on Gaza over the last five weeks has led to worldwide condemnation and outrage on a popular level, with repeated large-scale protests, marches, and other types of direct action happening all around the world in solidarity with Palestine. How important do you think this is? Do you think international solidarity can prove a significant factor in this struggle?

AO: Many think that solidarity with Palestine is a unidirectional action meant to provide Palestinians with support, a sense of psychological relief that our struggle does not meet deaf ears. I am more interested in the other side of the equation, on what the Palestinian struggle uncovers about the institutional, economic, and structural realities for those in the global north, the Arab world, and global south. To me the Palestinian struggle exposes truths, reveals fascisms, and emboldens trajectories of change, radical political, and economic change in these

societies – or at least it should do so. Palestine is not a nationalist, nor a religious, nor a feel-good cause. It is not simply a ceasefire movement. Our gift to the world [was] given through our blood, especially for those interested in a more just, more economically equal, decolonial, deracialised world. The struggle we lead reveals hidden discourses of imperialisms and forces centres of power to reveal their schizophrenic stances and hypocritical posturing. This is why Palestine is a universal struggle, a place for the condensation of truth in a post-truth historical conjecture. It is also a place from which the imperial metropole, and those within it suffering from racialised inequalities, can see in Palestine and its struggle a natural and political affinity. Historically the Palestinian struggle galvanised the left, and helped construct new modes of political engagements. This is precisely the reason why pro-Israel networks are attempting to shut down the discussion through fear and intimidation tactics.

Having said that, from a purely political perspective, the lack of consensus on a long war in Palestine, the energies of mobilisation across the globe, the reinvigoration of anti-war movements, are all central to pressures on political power and to reduce the temporal space given for the offensive Israeli action in the Gaza Strip.

LA: For understandable reasons, much of the world's eyes have mainly been focused on Gaza the last month but in that time Israel's violence has also increased in the West Bank where you are. Could you tell us a bit about what has been happening there since October 7th, and how this links into the broader struggle against Zionist settler colonialism in Palestine?

AO: In the West Bank, there are two distinct but intertwined struggles. The first is an armed resistance that incorporates popular actions against Israeli settlers and the military. The second is a political battle directed against the Palestinian Authority (PA).

While these conflicts are related, they also operate simultaneously and separately. The political unbinding from the PA is most evident among the working-class Palestinians in refugee camps, rural areas, and the old cities and is embodied in the creation of armed groups in some of these areas. This armed movement is often met with scepticism by the more dependent and politically disengaged upper and middle classes. Nonetheless, the PA is facing significant challenges. It is under pressure from these internal uprisings and a covert desire within the Israeli political spectrum – outspokenly represented by Ben Gvir and his settler movement – which suggests that even reliance on the PA and its security cooperation is a dependency that the Zionist movement ought to sever. This suggests a shift towards a more decisive military stance, aiming to displace Palestinians from their land. A third form of pressure arises from the indifference of American, European, and Arab stakeholders. The PA, adopting a wait and see strategy, could find itself at a disadvantage if the resistance in the Gaza Strip manages to endure and gain momentum.

Currently the Israeli army is conducting extensive operations in the West Bank. It is using its relative freedom of movement there to arrest and conduct special operations in self-defence zones in the North of the West Bank, such as Tul-Karem and Jenin. This is coupled with mass demonstrations and clashes by Palestinians in the West Bank. It has also engaged in a wide arrest campaign targeting political and social activists; since October 7th it has arrested over 2,000 Palestinians across the West Bank. Almost 200 Palestinians have been killed by the Israeli army and settlers in that time. More worryingly, the Israelis have also issued a wide arming campaign of settlers in the West Bank – officially inaugurating an active armed militia operating alongside the Israeli army in the West Bank.

LA: We recently published an article by Ameed Faleh in which he argues October 7th marks the 'permanent death' of the Oslo Accords. Would you share that sentiment? And if so, what do you think that means both for the West Bank specifically but also the future of the Palestinian Liberation movement generally?

AO: I align with the general direction of the analysis but reserve certainty, as I believe both relative victory and defeat are possible outcomes. It's conceivable that we may emerge from this conflict with the PA and the neoliberal political paradigm strengthened. There could be a collective shock on the Palestinian side that facilitates the replication of Dayton's security doctrine in the Gaza Strip. War is a transient moment, frozen in time. Although I am hopeful for a different outcome, we must recognise that Palestinians are a vulnerable people striving for survival. Their cooperation with, as well as resistance to, Israel are both anchored in the fundamental need to endure against forces that seek their eradication. These approaches are politically divergent but, at their core, are strategies for survival. The ongoing conflict in Gaza may compel Palestinians to commit more firmly to one form of survival strategy over the other.

LA: The extent to which Israel remains dependent on US military aid and support has been revealed very starkly over the last month, and it is clear that without it Israel is not a sustainable venture. There is clearly the risk of a large-scale regional war because of that, but do you think it's conceivable that Israel could eventually be perceived as a liability to US interests by a significant enough portion of the US ruling class that their relationship could be fundamentally reconsidered? And if so, what would the implications of that be?

AO: I doubt that America's ruling class will immediately acknowledge Israel as a strategic burden. Over the past two decades, we have heard scepticism about Israel's strategic value from voices close to the establishment – these include military and foreign policy experts from prestigious institutions, as well as professors and academics in the foreign policy worlds. Yet, it's crucial to recognise that the Israel lobby remains potent and influential and that the US for various historical, cultural, and electoral reasons will remain committed to Israel for the foreseeable future. A key argument of the lobby, and a component of America's stance in the region, has been the erroneous belief that the Palestinian issue is a foregone conclusion and irrelevant to global affairs. This perspective was challenged and could be further undermined if Israel fails to achieve its goals in the ongoing conflicts in Gaza and the West Bank.

But perhaps what is also highly significant is that Israel required America's military power to deter Hizbollah and Iran. Its self-proclaimed independence was exposed as a farce in front of its own society, but also within the domain of Zionist confidence that Israel is an embodiment of 'Jewish' independent power. Politically it also means that the US will be able to exercise more leverage on Israeli politics, on its long-term trajectories and on some of its internal policies and politics. It is not necessarily good news for Palestinians, but it shows the extent of Israel's dependency on American military industries, financial prowess, diplomatic clout and system of alliances in the region. It also indicates who has the upper hand in the relationship, reversing the notion that the road to Washington moves through Tel-Aviv or Jerusalem. In fact, it shows that Tel Aviv is an outpost for American power – one that remains fragile.

However, it is important to point out that despite what I have just laid out, the Israelis are using the events of 7th of October to leverage American and European power, to settle scores and attempt to redefine political and strategic realities.

LA: In spite of the horror of what we have witnessed over the last month and the ongoing human suffering in Gaza and elsewhere, I am convinced that what we are witnessing is the beginning of the end of the Zionist colonial project in Palestine. Do you think that is an overly optimistic or unrealistic assessment on my behalf or is that something you feel could be the case too?

AO: One crucial lesson for the world to recognise is that the Palestinian struggle is intergenerational; it persists regardless of the immediate outcomes. Palestinians will persistently seek fissures to exploit, forge new paths, establish organisations, and mobilise their cultural, social, economic, and technological resources to reclaim their land. There is an unyielding will to continue, even when the tide seems to turn against them or when defeat appears to become systemic. The only answer to this indefatigable pursuit is justice. Indeed, the current conflict is a significant and pivotal moment in this enduring endeavour, and it will be a marker of what is yet to come in the long term.

Currently, there are several indicators that support your analysis. Palestine is emerging as an urgent issue on the global stage. Additionally, the Palestinian resistance has formed an active alliance system which is strategically complicating Israel's offensive operations in the Gaza Strip. Israel is also enduring economic, political, and psychological tolls, which are fostering an immediate willingness to sacrifice but are simultaneously forcing it to grapple with the limits of its influence and capabilities. While the outcomes will hinge on the conflict's progression and the potential for escalation in the region, various early signs suggest that Israel could be facing setbacks which transcend the events of October 7th.

Israel's strategic objectives in Gaza appear disoriented. Despite some tactical successes, it remains to be seen how these will translate into long-term strategic gains within the limited timeframe available for military operations. It's important to note that the American political and military engagement in the region does not align with Israel's operational timeline in Gaza. Israel's approach has been cautious and slow, seemingly unable to decisively overcome Palestinian resistance, which is strategically prolonging the conflict. It is prepared for a drawn-out struggle, conserving its resources and personnel for a sustained defensive battle rather than a short-term confrontation. Claims of deterring Hizbullah and Iran are, at best, temporary; the strategic calculations in Beirut and Tehran could shift quickly if no diplomatic resolutions emerge and redlines are crossed. While American and British citizens might be indifferent to the Palestine-Israel conflict, they are concerned about domestic issues such as rising inflation, economic decline, and the prospect of their soldiers being drawn into conflicts on the behest of Israel.

This is why the US is urging Israel to intensify and expedite its military operations. However, Israel is not only concerned about the potential backlash from civilian casualties but also fears that significant military losses could adversely affect public sentiment within the country. Currently, Israel is mobilising over 360,000 reserve soldiers and is also dealing with an influx of Israelis from the Gaza envelope and the borders with Lebanon. More than 200,000 Israelis are awaiting their return home. The situation is taking a substantial economic toll, affecting sectors like tourism, agriculture, restaurants, bars, and high-tech companies, many of whose employees are now engaged in military service. The escalating pressure from Hizbullah is compelling Israel to face tough decisions about whether to expand the war and use this moment of unity and willingness to sacrifice to confront Hizbullah or to de-escalate. Not to mention the pressure placed by the families of Israelis held by Palestinian groups in the Gaza Strip. Maintaining such a level of mobilisation without clear victories will prove difficult to sustain in the medium run.

These are all indications that currently Israel is looking for an image of victory, one that can give Israel and their military and intelligence apparatus some respite from the events of the 7th of October.

LA: Thank you so much for offering us your time and crucial analysis, Abdaljawad. Is there anything else you would like to add that we haven't already touched on?

AO: Thank you, Louis. An important aspect that should be mentioned is the vehement attacks on pro-Palestinian voices. The conflation of antisemitism with the rejection of ethno-nationalist fascism would be almost amusing if it weren't so tragic. Recently, we have seen Christian Zionists, who harbour deeply antisemitic views, join forces with right-wing Zionists from the Jewish community in demonstrations in Washington DC. This alliance illustrates that the weaponisation of Jewish memory of precariousness and vulnerability is alive, but that in a tragic twist that weaponisation can sit comfortably with actual antisemites. Moreover, it shows that discourses of antisemitism are not only tools used to silence pro-Palestinian voices but are also aimed at undermining Jewish and progressive support for Palestinians and their struggle. The fear created by banning student organisations, going after public figures supportive of Palestinian rights, is an Orwellian moment par excellence. Today, true courage involves speaking out despite the fears, continuously engaging in critical examination, and refusing to let any subject become taboo. This includes the criticism and understanding of Palestinian resistance, its history, evolution, and political wager.

Abdaljawad Omar is a writer, analyst, and lecturer based in Ramallah, Palestine. He currently lectures in the Department of Philosophy and Cultural Studies at Birzeit University.

Louis Allday is a writer and historian. He is the Founding Editor of Liberated Texts *and an Editor at* Ebb.

Al-Aqsa Flood: Imperialism, Zionism and Reactionism in the 21st Century

Hassan Harb

On October 7, 2023, between 2-3,000 Palestinian fighters from various political factions, including Hamas, Palestinian Islamic Jihad, the DFLP (Democratic Front for the Liberation of Palestine) and the PFLP (Popular Front for the Liberation of Palestine) among others, broke the 16-year-old siege of Gaza. They did so to launch an epic battle in the Southern occupied-territory of historic Palestine in an attempt to ignite a war of liberation from the yoke of the Zionist entity (Israel). We have now entered the eighth day of the war, which has witnessed the immediate and unanimous condemnation of the Palestinians by the collective West, who rushed to protect Israel's right to defend itself. Singling out Hamas as the only faction leading the battle, the collective Western ruling classes coalesced in labelling this historic operation an Islamic-inspired 'terrorist operation'. The portrayal of Palestinians as Islamic terrorists provided the necessary green light for the Israeli government to bomb Gaza incessantly and prepare for a ground invasion. The collective West has shown absolute unity and support to genocidal Israeli calls for 'wiping Gaza out' and cutting off their gas, water, and electricity, while the Israeli PM, Benjamin Netanyahu, proudly posted on Twitter/X the bombing of a civilian residence in the Gaza Strip.

The drums of war continue, the Palestinian fighters are still engaged in the battle and, as the Palestinian factions in the West Bank have begun to confront the occupation forces, other regional players, such as Iran, Syria, and Hezbollah, might join the war at any moment. In this piece, I attempt to reflect on the scale and significance of the war both regionally and globally, drawing upon the theoretical tools that have often guided people of the Global South to understand their plight and struggles. That is, I believe it is important to go back to the conceptual triad of Imperialism-Zionism-Reactionism to situate this historic battle beyond the mere confines of the open-air prison of Gaza. In doing so, we must draw on these concepts, yet upgrade them to the present times, to understand the dialectical nature of this war in a world that is witnessing the slow (yet steady) decline of US-led imperialism.

Imperialism: The end of the unipolar moment of the US

Imperialism refers to a world system of surplus value extraction,[1] where development is apportioned unequally along racial and class lines. It is a set of material relations of exploitation between countries of the Global

North and South, which takes place through a process of class collaboration between ruling classes in the core and compradors in the periphery. Accumulation then depends more and more on the degree that imperialist countries oppress and exploit developing countries.[2]

This entails, for instance, the use of military domination and policies that prevent developing countries from harnessing their internal resources for the purpose of regional or popular development. At the same time, this historically established unequal accumulation of wealth does not only entail the pile of commodities and natural resources, but it is also the mass of ideas corresponding to capital's encroaching logic. In other words, imperialism as a sociological phenomenon[3] operates as both a material and ideological process.

In the aftermath of WWII, it was the US that consolidated its political and financial leverage worldwide, becoming the major imperialist power. As a creditor to France and Britain during the war, the US attempted to restructure the world system in the wake of the deficit-driven withdrawals of European colonialism from Africa and Asia.[4] This task was predicated on the interrelated realms of trade and military expansion. On matters of trade, the post-war Truman Administration sought to establish an 'Open Door', with 'the elimination of trade and financial barriers, exclusive trading blocs, and restrictive policies of every sort'.[5] While portraying these new trade arrangements as facilitating a neutral freedom of enterprise and international exchange, they in fact represented an Americanisation of the global system, reflecting US capital's needs as they existed in the late 1940s. The newly created World Bank and International Monetary Fund (IMF) regulated world trade under a common currency of the US dollar; the post-war economic reconstruction of Western Europe provided US exporters with emergent markets; and military coordination with a declining British imperialism allowed US corporations preferential access to the key resources of the industrialised world, namely oil. Inevitably, it was the mythology of "American exceptionalism" that helped maintain these policies of domination. This political mythology incarnated the missionary and colonial zeal that justified the genocide of the Americas[6] and displayed a religious belief towards the idea that the US has a unique role to play in world history, while other countries would follow.

However, the progressive economic rise of China and two Russian military interventions, respectively in support of the Syrian government in 2015 and against NATO encroachment in Ukraine in 2022, have decisively thrown the US and its allies, Europe and Japan, into a geopolitical nightmare. US-led imperialism has entered an historical phase of political decline. The unipolar moment is crumbling, whereas new political blocs from the Global South, such as the BRICS, are becoming more assertive in shaping an international order that prevents their humiliation, but rather treats them equally. Together with these processes, we also witnessed a wave of military coups in West Africa against French/Western neocolonialism, and the increasing assertiveness of Iran in West Asia and its collaboration with Russia, while Cuba and Venezuela withstood decades of sanctions and US-sponsored coups. The pressure on US-led imperialism and its allies is increasing, and the most immediate reaction to the conscious realisation of their decline has been a renewed wave of blatant fascist rhetoric and ideology. Starting with the 2016 election of Donald Trump in the US, the most striking feature of newly fascist Europe has been the complete rehabilitation of Nazism in Ukraine as a form of popular resistance against 'dictatorial' Russia. From Giorgia Meloni in Italy to Emmanuel Macron in France, the European ruling classes are ready to sacrifice their people and countries at all costs for the mighty US.

Zionism and Reactionism: From Arab Unity to the Muqawama

In such a context, the Arab region has occupied a unique role in the geostrategy of US-led imperialism since WWII, especially due to its oil wealth. Being a key natural resource for the economies of the imperialist countries, the best means of ensuring this guaranteed access consisted in securing political control of the region.[7] To achieve these goals, US-led imperialism operated in close cooperation with two faithful allies – Israel and the reactionary Gulf monarchies.

As for the Zionist entity, this became effectively a US military outpost in the region.[8] As Sheila Ryan[9] writes, from 1948 until mid-1973 'Israel had received the staggering sum of over $8 billion in economic assistance from various foreign sources, or $3,500 total for each Israeli – an average of $233 per year per capita in aid. Thus, an average Israeli each year received in aid alone more than double the per capita income of an Egyptian ($102 in 1969)'. Between 1943 and 2023, the US has provided Israel with $160 billion in aid (with inflation adjusted reaching about $260 billion),[10] without considering the regular loan guarantees extended to the entity that are worth billions. This aid to Israel is an investment in militarism for US-led imperialism. The peculiarity of the Zionist entity lies in it being a settler-colonial formation, as much as the US, incubating a mode of consciousness that promotes imperialist values and secures US hegemonic domination in the region. By acquiring nuclear weapons and through its numerous military attacks on and invasions of other countries of the region – i.e., such as Iraq,[11] Lebanon, Syria,[12] Israel has been the major force behind imperialist capital accumulation and its corollary, Arab de-development. As the Palestinian leftist circles in the 1960s-70s consistently emphasised, Zionism is the spearhead of imperialism in the region. As much as the liberation of Palestine is a struggle against US-led imperialism on whose behalf Israel acts as a gendarme, an attack on Israel is an attempt to undermine directly the core interests of the US and its reactionary allies in the region.

As per the oil-rich Gulf monarchies, the control of the ruling classes of these political formations guaranteed the supremacy of the US dollar at the international level through dollar-denominated oil sales,[13] which were then being recycled in the purchase of US treasury bonds and weaponry. In recent years, following the various attacks on the sovereignty of secular Arab republics (Iraq, Libya, and Syria), coordinated with the money and weapons of the Gulf countries, the US has also pushed an agenda of normalisation with Israel. The more Israel is recognised officially in the region, the more secure the interests of US-led imperialism are.

However, two more processes unfolded whichshook the geopolitical equilibrium of the region. First, while 2011 witnessed the success of NATO-led regime change operation in Libya, Russia's 2015 intervention in Syria - itself spurred in part by its experiences with the Libya invasion - showed that regional and geopolitical balances had changed. Second, the capacity of the Islamic Republic of Iran to withstand decades of sanctions (as Cuba, the Democratic People's Republic of Korea (DPRK) and Venezuela have done) has allowed it to grow into an important political player in the region, becoming the number one enemy of the Zionist entity. Providing support to other socio-political formations in the region, including Hezbollah in Lebanon and Ansar Allah in Yemen, the political and military assertiveness of Iran represents a decisive shift in the nature of the ideological march of the region against Zionism. With the consolidation of the *muqawama* (Resistance) ideology, both Iran and Hezbollah have largely avoided producing a sectarian, exclusionary, Shia-led vision for the region. In other words, they circumvented the danger of responding with the same medicine to what US-led imperialism had progressively funded – since the times of the Afghan mujahedeen – working hand-in-hand with Sunni reactionary forces. On the contrary, the *muqawama* has dialectically preserved the historical and ideological continuity of the region, moving from Arab to Muslim unity. It did not reject the past *a priori*. It has instead combined the past with the present, creating a new ideological order that calls on the Arab, Islamic identity of the region to fight against the material and ideological war unleashed by foreign oppressors on the sovereignty of every state in the region. As Seyed Hassan Nasrallah once remarked:

> In the project of American hegemony … it is not permitted for a strong state to exist … a strong state in the sense of an independent state, a state that makes its decisions on its own, a country that takes into account the interests of its people, a country that benefits from and employs its resources and its economy, a state that develops scientifically, technically, culturally and administratively at every level. In the project of American hegemony [such a state] is forbidden.

Witnessing the decline of the unipolar world order, the *muqawama* incarnates an Axis of Defence that stands firmly to ward off imperialist attacks on the region. It also could create the space for future and unexpected realignments. In fact, while mainstream analyses saturated the Western public with a picture of a Sunni-Shia divide, positing Saudi Arabia against Iran, as defining the region and seemingly having to shape its future, it was the People's Republic of China that scored an important political move brokering a diplomatic deal between these two countries in 2023. What if Iran and Saudi could shape a common path together in the future for the region?

That said, reactionism is still alive and kicking in the region. The interests of the ruling classes of various comprador regimes continue to be closely connected to US-led

imperial capital, especially Jordan, Egypt and UAE. Yet, Al-Aqsa Flood has accelerated these contradictions existing between the reactionary states of the region and their people, as well as within the emerging multipolar order. Whereas the UAE had already normalised with the Zionist entity, Saudi Arabia is now responding by freezing any future discussion around normalisation, while liaising (for the first time) with Iran over the situation. In this regard, Al-Aqsa Flood could become the graveyard of the US-backed transportation corridor, hoping to link India via Saudi Arabia and Israel to the EU. Unsurprisingly, India rushed to support Israel, but far more powerful BRICS members had complete opposite reactions. On a phone call with their Brazilian counterparts, the Chinese Foreign Ministry did not hesitate to highlight how "the crux of the issue lies in the fact that justice has not been done to the Palestinian people."[14] The unfolding of these events is increasingly bad news for the US and its hopes to 'withdraw' from the region in order to focus on China. The Palestinians have struck a direct blow to US core interests. They not only opened a new and unexpected military front, but also reminded the Global South that the creation of a new world order must pass through Palestine, unless the power of the US remains unchallenged.

Also, Al-Aqsa Flood has accentuated further the existing gap between the reactionary ruling regimes and their constituencies. Regardless of the interests of the compradors, they do not reflect those of the working masses of the region. As the Jordanian military miserably cordoned the border with Israel, when the Resistance called for major mobilisations across the region, people still flocked to the borders in support of Palestine. What Al-Aqsa Flood has unleashed is a reignition in the region's working class consciousness of how interconnected their fate is to the struggle against US capital, its military bases, and reactionary allies. This is a process that is slowly unfolding and its shape and intensity remain to be seen. For example, Lebanese protesters' attack on McDonalds in Saida manifests an early example of mass mobilisation against the ideological and material incarnations of US-led imperialism in the region. In Alexandria, the shooting of two Israeli tourists and the discourse it propagated about Israelis as enemies of the Arab nation is a further blow to the official Egyptian stance on normalisation. This means that the fight is not simply about or in Gaza; rather it is taking place in all Arab capitals–from Cairo to Amman and Baghdad–and for the working masses of the region to organise themselves around Palestine is to regain their future and independence.

Gaza is the world's hope for a just future

In such a context, there are several elements that we must consider when looking at the Palestinian operation launched on October 7, 2023. First, the operation represents the Palestinians' way to enter decisively in this historical moment of US decline, launching a war of liberation against the Zionist entity that, like the *muqawama*, combines the past and present towards the future. Choosing the 50th anniversary of the Arab War on Israel in 1973, the Al-Aqsa Flood Palestinian war of liberation builds on the past Arab Unity yet projects itself toward a future that calls for all Arabs, Muslim and Christians, to fight for and defend the holy sites.[15] At the same time, while the nature and scale of Al-Aqsa Flood is undoubtedly historical, its capacity to magnetise and coalesce militarily the Arab masses around the fight for liberation of Palestine is not immediate. A concrete obstacle remains–as mentioned above–due to the reactionary regimes of the region, whose core interests are tied to US-led capital, without forgetting the systematic military destruction that has ravaged the major anti-Zionist republics of the region (Iraq, Libya, and Syria). Yet, the Axis of *muqawama* cannot lose its allies in Palestine. In fact, Hezbollah has repeatedly warned that it is ready to enter the war, should a ground invasion of Gaza take place. This reveals the cumulative character of history. We cannot approach Al-Aqsa Flood solely as the final road to a war of liberation, but as one of the major steps that – starting with the 2006 military victory of Hezbollah against Israel – will lead to the ploughing of the crops in the liberation field.

Second, the Zionist entity has been taken completely by surprise. The most technologically advanced army of the region has failed to prevent such an attack, and this already represents a major political loss. Crossed by increasing societal contradictions that posit liberal and conservative settlers against each other, Netanyahu hopes to unite the country around what represents Israel the most: the Genocide of Palestinians. For these reasons, numerous Israeli politicians have called openly for a second Nakba, aiming to wipe Gaza off the earth. However, these genocidal calls are a pyrrhic victory for the Zionists, since they only manifest further to Global South countries the quick descent of the West and its allies into moral and political fascism. At the same time, genocidal calls could also meet another fate. That is, should the West Bank decide to raise up in arms and join the factions in Gaza, or the Axis of *muqawama* decide to open new military fronts, Israel could find itself completely cornered. A full onslaught of Gaza by the Zionist entity – as explained above – is a reassertion of a declining US power in the region. In other words, it proceeds against historical time, since both Russia, China and the various countries of the Global South are all watching the war, and Palestine represents a test to their new desire to shape an equal global order.

Third, this dialectical movement is incomprehensible for the so-called Western Leftists, who cannot reconcile themselves with the idea that a progressive fight in the region has taken an Islamic-led turn - even while, as described above, the ideologically heterogenous resistance forces in Palestine have embraced strategic coordination and alliances with the likes of Hamas. Blinded by their imperialist arrogance, the collective West has either slid very quickly into fascist and fanatical support for Israel, or found its leftist groups completely disoriented. The latter, in fact, continues to look desperately for the 'right' amount or type of violence and, when not present, it rushes to condemn both sides equally. It goes without saying that, after having normalised and supported seven decades of Zionist violence over the Palestinians and successive bombings of the region, the West is failing itself as an ally of Palestine at this historical juncture. To put it interrogatively: has the Western left, despite all its opposition, ever managed to prevent a US or NATO-led bombing in the region? In this critical historical moment, the Western left should be reminded that Gaza and the struggle for Palestine is humanity's hope for a better world. The past few days have shown how the collective Western civil, educational, and media institutions work hand-in-hand with their military and security apparatuses, all of them deployed to protect the interests of the ruling classes. Time is ripe for the Western Left to mobilise on many fronts, respectively for the short and long term: 1) to counter the unanimous genocidal support that their ruling classes are providing to the Zionist entity; 2) to provide a political alternative that joins the South in creating an alternative and more equitable world order. As Ghassan Kanafani, Palestinian author and leading member of the PFLP, famously wrote: 'The Palestinian Cause is not a cause for Palestinians only, but a cause for every revolutionary, wherever he is … a cause of the exploited and oppressed masses'.

Al-Aqsa Flood is a moment that incarnates our historical time. The Palestinian, Arab and Muslim masses have decided to enter the stage and tell the world that they will not be left out of history. They are ready to join the fight for a more equal world for the majority of its inhabitants. Are you?

References

1   See Arghiri Emmanuel, *Unequal Exchange: A Study of the Imperialism of Trade* (Monthly Review Press, 1972); Samir Amin, *Unequal Development: An Essay on the Social Formations of Peripheral Capitalism* (Monthly Review Press, 1976); Utsa Patnaik and Prabhat Patnaik, *A Theory of Imperialism* (Columbia University Press, 2016).

2   Ali Kadri, *Imperialism with Reference to Syria* (Springer, 2019).

3   Anouar Abdel-Malek, *Social Dialectics: Nation and Revolution* (SUNY Press, 1981).

4   Joyce Kolko and Gabriel Kolko, *The Limits of Power: The World and United States Foreign Policy, 1945-1954* (Harper & Row, 1972).

5   Joyce Kolko and Gabriel Kolko, *The Limits of Power*, 12.

6   Domenico Losurdo, *Il marxismo occidentale. Come nacque, come morì, come può rinascere* [Western marxism: How it was born, how it died, how it can be reborn] (Bari: Laterza, 2017).

7   Brandon Wolfe-Hunnicutt, *The Paranoid Style in American Diplomacy: Oil and Arab Nationalism in Iraq* (Stanford: Stanford University Press, 2021).

8   Seif Dana, 'The Setback 49: The Dialectic of Neoliberalism and War', *Wattan* , 2016.

9   Sheila Ryan, 'Israeli Economic Policy in the Occupied Areas: Foundations of a New Imperialism', *MERIP Reports* (1974) 24, 6.

10   Jeremy M. Sharp, 'US Foreign Aid to Israel', *Congressional Research Service* (2023).

11   Soula Avramidis, 'Iraq's Constitution: The Dream of "New Imperialism"', *Monthly Review* (2005).

12   Patrick Higgins, 'Gunning for Damascus: The US war on the Syrian Arab Republic', *Middle East Critique* 32:3, (2023).

13   Max Ajl, *A People's Green New Deal* (Pluto Press, 2021).

14   Yukio Tajima, 'China calls lack of justice for Palestinians "crux" of conflict', *Nikkei Asia*, 2023.

15   Hamas, 'Statement for the People', *Resistance News Network*, 9 October 2023.

October 7th: The Permanent Death of the Oslo Accords

Ameed Faleh

'Destroy them, destroy them, this time, Israel must destroy Hamas, otherwise we're done'
– An unnamed Palestinian Authority official to an Israeli researcher after Israel announced its post-October 7th siege of the Gaza Strip[1]

Hamas' surprise military assault on the settlements of the so-called 'Gaza Envelope' on October 7th shocked everyone by the scale, ingenuity, and speed of which it was conducted. From paramotors to bulldozers, Hamas, even for a few hours, forcefully broke Gaza's 16-year siege. Its fighters arrested Israeli settlers for a potential prisoner swap and put Israel's Gaza Division effectively out of service. This victory should not be viewed only in a military sense; its political connotations threaten the neoliberal peace paradigm that Israel, the US, and the EU pushed, often through a combination of soft and hard power tactics.

This paradigm, upon which the 1993 Oslo Accords are hinged, forced the creation of a 'peace dividend,' an incentive for the still-nascent Palestinian Authority (hereafter PA) to uphold its end of the bargain – that is, security and economic obligations towards Israel and maintaining the PA's control over the scattered towns and refugee camps that it controls. This dividend is described by Pal-estinian researcher Toufic Haddad as 'rents [...] ultimately enforced by Israel, in the hopes that a workable social, political and economic order [in favor of Israel] could be forged across the OPT.'[2] The term 'subcontractor' is often used to describe the PA's subservience to Western and Israeli interests in favor of keeping the steady supply of the 'peace dividends' flowing. A subcontractor, however, has contractual obligations as well as rights; meanwhile, the PA, in Israeli eyes, does not have any rights which extend past nourishing its role as a perpetual 'interim' self-governing authority relieving the occupation from its obligations vis-a-vis directly ruling the colonised. As such, the term 'proxy' is more apt in the case of the PA.

Capitalist neoliberal development in the West Bank and the Gaza Strip was encouraged by the UN, the World Bank, and the International Monetary Fund. This mirage of development, dubbed by political economist Sara Roy as 'de-development,'[3] uprooted any hopes for genuine national development in the 1967 territories, steering it towards further erosion of Palestinian agriculture and small-scale industry in favor of certain facades of autonomy. Gaza International Airport, which served flights exclusively within the Arab World, could simply be put out of operation via an Israeli order or an artillery strike, as was done permanently in 2002.

Rawabi, the first Palestinian-planned city which is built on the land of nearby expropriated villages and is inspired by the Israeli settlement of Modi'in,[4] shows the grotesque intersection of the PLO's nationalist discourse with the neoliberal peace paradigm pushed onto Palestinians. Amir Dajani, the project manager of Rawabi, described the position of the Palestinian bourgeoisie under Oslo: '[w]e are in the business of moderation, building harmony, coexistence, supporting the visionary two-state solution that is hoping to be the way forward under the circumstances [...] [We are] not in the business of politics, [we are] in the business of job creation.'[5] As such, job creation, real estate, and extravagant multi-million dollar projects adopt a faux-liberatory aspect that is depoliticised by its enablers and creators. They nevertheless serve a political purpose of creating a certain strata of Palestinian society that benefits directly from the status-quo. Individualist progress is thus portrayed as a step towards securing statehood.

Touching upon the security side, the peace dividend put forth by 'the international community' in order to subdue the PLO rests purely on guaranteeing the status-quo at all costs and on the creation of patrimonial networks within Palestinian society, irrespective of what their views on the PA might be, to cement that society's reliance on Oslo despite constant Israeli settler colonial expansion. It is not a surprise to see that with the signing of the Declaration of Principles (DOP)[6] in 1993, many hardline members of Fatah[7] in Gaza and the West Bank swiftly adopted the peace process discourse: it materially benefitted them, despite many of them still being in Israeli crosshairs. A statement put forth by Fatah Hawks in the Gaza Strip, the armed wing of Fatah during the First Intifada, after the signing of the DOP and the discovery of an Israeli hit list that targeted them, unveiled the new discourse that prevailed using the patrimonial networks of the PA/PLO: 'Israel wants our sole representative, the PLO, to condemn terrorism, but it exercises terrorism against those who defend the agreement that was signed between Israel and the PLO.'[8] This statement effectively embodied the role of the patrimonial networks of the PA/PLO as defenders and upholders of the newly-created status quo. The assassination of Ahmad Abu Rish, a local Fatah Hawks leader, after he was supposedly granted amnesty by the Occupation through the PA, highlighted the fragility of the state-building narrative. In addition, the 1996 torture and killing of prominent Nablus-based Fatah Hawks leader, Mahmoud Ejemayyel, in PA custody for his refusal to give up his arms, underscores the PA's desire to guarantee total adherence to its statebuilding narrative – even at the expense of killing other Fatah leaders for disobedience.

In recent times, the PA's role as the upholder of the Oslo status-quo was shaken by Hamas's 2007 takeover of the Gaza Strip and the growth of the resistance factions there. The PA, barely surviving the Second Intifada intact, aimed to contrast its supposed economic growth and tightened security grip with the Israeli-engineered institutionalised impoverishment[9] of the Gaza Strip. In essence, both Israel and the PA were working with each other to demonise and criminalise resistance in the eyes of the population of the West Bank, while facilitating the influx of foreign investment in real estate and luxury projects. This carrot was accompanied by the stick: the torture of Palestinians detained in Jericho Prison has become notorious, as has the continued aggressions against and the increasingly cruel blockade of the Gaza Strip. This alliance to thwart the Palestinian Resistance is made even clearer in the recent statements of a PA official calling for the continued bombardment of the Palestinians in Gaza following the Al Aqsa Flood operation.

The types of discourse of which the PA, and by extension Fatah, used to demonise Hamas varied, but have mainly rested upon the Islamist nature of the movement. Fatah is juxtaposed as the more 'rational' actor when it comes to taking socio-political decisions. In addition, the PA used the alliance between Iran, Hamas and the Palestinian Islamic Jihad as alleged proof that both factions were simply Iranian 'pawns', disregarding its own infamous Dayton battalions[10] and continued reliance on politically-motivated foreign donor aid. The 'Iranian puppet' card is malicious in how it props up the American and Gulf-sponsored demonisation campaign of resistance movements across the Arab World. A common talking point, for example, is to paint Hezbollah as taking orders directly from Tehran with no agency. It is also a projection by the PA: its elites and patrons cannot imagine genuine state allyship with any political project without Palestinians being at the weak end of the bargain.

These sentiments did not start with Iran. In the late 1960s, Ghassan Kanafani wrote an article under the pseudonym of Faris Faris criticising this very phenomenon: an Arab liberal attacked Gamal Abdel Nasser and accused him of being a Soviet puppet, describing the Fedayeen as 'janissaries aligned with the Soviet Empire.'[11] This removal of agency is also dehumanisation. Again, for the PA and the US, the 'bad' Palestinians are never rational actors acting in their own interests.

How does this tie into today? October 7th, and the rise of resistance groups in the West Bank before it, exposed the futility of the statebuilding process that the PA espouses. Settlements expand, settler attacks in the West Bank increase exponentially, hope for any political solution with the PA is crushed time and time again. In the heyday of Yasser Arafat and Salam Fayyad, increased securitisation and the PA's role as a security proxy were justified on the basis of a political settlement: the Interim period, Camp David, and Annapolis.

Today, the PA lacks any political legitimacy to mask its role as a second South Lebanon Army[12] for Israel. The continued theft of land and the denial of rights of the refugees of the Gaza Strip, as well as the rest of the Palestinians, bestowed a duty upon Hamas and the resistance factions to launch the attack to break the status-quo. Oslo failed to free the Palestinian prisoners as promised by PLO officials, and the right of return was similarly sidelined; the Great March of Return in 2018 was crushed by the kneecapping of protestors in their hundreds. The international community cheered on, hoping to trap both Gaza and the West Bank with its own standards of passive resistance, statebuilding, and individualist economic prosperity that hides itself behind the veil of a collective effort to produce the New Palestinian[13] to the world.

The significance of the October 7th assault thus becomes clearer: it was an attack not only against Israeli settler colonialism, but also against the fundamental discourse that underlies the PA. It broke the taboo on centering Palestinian rights through the lens of decolonial and revolutionary armed struggle. More importantly, it scathed the colonial hubris of a nuclear-armed beast that boasts of its weaponry and supposed military superiority to the world when 'mowing the lawn' in Gaza. No wonder, then, why the international community is cheering on the destruction of Gaza and the elimination of resistance. Out of fear that Hamas would break the perpetual stalemate that the PLO signed on to in 1993, the US wants to quench the Zionist bloodthirst that ensued after October 7th through JDAMS,[14] Delta Force squadrons, and a media clergy[15] that parrots every Israeli army claim that demonises not only the Resistance, but the entire population of Gaza. The entire Israeli political spectrum is united around portraying Palestinians as Nazis, ISIS members, 'children of darkness', as well as human animals in order to manufacture worldwide consent for the continuous bombardment of the Gaza Strip.

It is already clear that October 7th will become a landmark moment in the history of Palestinian resistance against Zionism, its benefactors, and its local agents. The PA, US, and Europe are encouraging the massacre and total siege of the Gaza Strip, not only because of their inherent interest in the continued existence of Israel on Arab land, but also because of their frenzied desire to try and restore the status quo, an imagined reality that existed before October 7th. Attempts to soften Hamas' position on liberation via the Quartet and Qatar never bore fruit, as evidenced by what has transpired since. The failure of the peace dividends to thwart the Palestinian people, the collapse of the political discourse that masks securitisation behind a national goal, and the continued will of the resistance groups in Gaza to fight despite an international siege and soft power tactics to entice them to stay silent – all of this will pave the way for a more revolutionary discourse with regards to liberation. The era of pseudo-statebuilding is finally behind us, and an age of liberation is coming.

Ameed Faleh is a Palestinian student at al-Quds University.

References

1   Ivana Kottasová, 'As a Ground Incursion Looms, the Big Question Remains: What Is Israel's Plan for Gaza?' *CNN*, October 21, 2023.

2   Toufic Haddad, *Palestine Ltd.: Neoliberalism and Nationalism in the Occupied Territory* (I.B. Taurus, 2018), 147.

3   For a thorough explanation of de-development pre-Oslo: Sara Roy 'The Gaza Strip: A Case of Economic De-Development', *Journal of Palestine Studies*, 17:1, (1987). For an explanation on what de-development entailed Post-Oslo: Sara Roy, "De-Development Revisited: Palestinian Economy and Society Since Oslo", *Journal of Palestine Studies*, 28:3 (1999).

4   For references to the Rawabi-Modi'in connection: Kareem Rabie, *Palestine is throwing a party and the whole world is invited: Capital and state building in the West Bank* (Duke University Press, 2021), 60-62.

5   Kareem Rabie, *Palestine is Throwing a Party,* 56

6   The Declaration of Principles was signed on September 13th, 1993, between the PLO and Israel in Washington, D.C. As per the agreement, the PLO recognised Israel's existence. The Declaration of Principles laid the groundwork for future interim period agreements and institutionalised the Palestinian Authority's existence.

7   The Palestinian National Liberation Movement (Fatah) is the largest faction that governs both the Palestine Liberation Organisation as well as the Palestinian Authority. It cemented its hegemony over the PLO after the resignation of Ahmad al-Shuqeiri, its founder, in 1969.

8   Azmi Mreish, *Quwwat al-Amn al-Watani al-Filastini: Al-Shurta al-Filastiniyya* [The Palestinian National Security Forces: the Palestinian Police]. (Abu Arafeh Publishing, 1993), 165.

9   The term 'institutionalised impoverishment' was adopted by Trude Strand as a theoretical framework to describe Israel's siege on Gaza since 2007. See: Trude Strand, 'Tightening the Noose: The Institutionalised Impoverishment of Gaza, 2005–2010', *Journal of Palestine Studies*, 43:2 (2014).

10   Dayton's Battalions refer to the PA forces that were trained under the auspices of the United States Security Coordinator, Keith Dayton.

11   Ghassan Kanafani, *Faris Faris: Kitabat Sakhira* [Faris Faris: Satirical Writings]. (Dar al-Adab, 1996), 52-53.

12   The South Lebanon Army (known locally in Lebanon as Lahd's Army) was a proxy militia founded by Saad Haddad that governed parts of South Lebanon. Armed and trained by Israel, it protected Israel's occupation of South Lebanon through brutal force. It saw its end with the liberation of South Lebanon in 2000 with Antoine Lahd, its leader, fleeing to Tel Aviv and living the last of his days in France.

13   Keith Dayton, the United States Security Coordinator responsible for training the forces of the PA after the Second Intifada infamously dubbed this term. See: 'D2. U.S. Security Coordinator Keith Dayton, Address Detailing the Mission and Accomplishments of the Office of the U.S. Security Coordinator, Israel and the Palestinian Authority, Washington, 7 May 2009 (Excerpts)', *Journal of Palestine Studies*, 38:4 (2009).

14   JDAMS are kits designed to transform unguided fighter jet bombs into high-precision missiles. The US routinely supplies Israel with these kits.

15   Samir Amin dubbed the term 'media clergy' to describe the stranglehold that media has on Western society and its role as the sole arbiter of truth via its class character. See: *Samir Amin, The Implosion of Contemporary Capitalism* (Monthly Review Press, 2013).

Two Logics of War: Liberation Against Genocide

Bikrum Gill

The onslaught of Western and Israeli propaganda since the beginning of Al-Aqsa Flood seeks to confuse and misrepresent what are in fact the very clear terms of the struggle in Palestine. The conflict between coloniser and colonised, between occupier and occupied, has reached now, finally and openly, a permanent overarching 'state of war' that contains within it a decisive confrontation between two particular logics of war. On one side, the Palestinian resistance has been undertaking a rising anti-colonial war of national liberation to free themselves and their lands from both Israeli colonialism and the larger Western imperial world order. On the other side stands an openly genocidal Israeli colonial project aiming to restore the colonial foundations that have been called into question by the Palestinian liberation war. It is in the increasingly evident incapacity of the Israeli army to defeat the Palestinian armed resistance on the battlefield that we can find the dark impetus for the Israeli and Western return to an openly genocidal approach that directs the violence of the colonial state towards the unarmed Palestinian population. Though the Israeli colonial war of genocide will not succeed in its aim of eliminating Palestinians from Gaza, it unleashes massacres and destruction on a horrific scale.

The logic of the war of national liberation is centred upon overturning the material equation of force that underpins colonialism and the broader imperialist world order. Here, colonialism and imperialism are premised, in the first and last instance, on a 'greater violence' that enables the coloniser to usurp sovereignty from the colonised. This material equation of force generates a secondary ideological projection of power wherein the coloniser appears as invincible in any encounter with the colonised, capable of enacting any degree of violence with impunity. The ideological legitimation of this impunity consists of a supposed higher rational purpose (e.g. anti-terror, civilisational, democracy promoting, humanitarian, etc.) that is ascribed to the coloniser's violence. The colonised, by contrast, are rendered as inherently killable in any contestation with the coloniser due to an irrational savagery that is attached to their violence. There is no higher rational purpose to be found here, only violence for the sake of a savagery that threatens all of humanity. Insofar as the colonised remain within such a balance of material and ideological force, they will by necessity be compelled to seek, or perhaps put more properly, beg for, recognition of their rights under the sovereign power of the coloniser. This is the condition to which Israel consigned the Palestinians with the Oslo Accords 'peace process' framework.

The total inability of the Oslo road to enforce Palestinian national rights and defend at any level Palestinian life and land created the conditions for a return of forms of armed resistance capable of calling into question the equation of force underpinning the denial of Palestinian sovereignty. The evolution of the post-Oslo armed resistance into a highly effective hybrid army, combining guerrilla tactics with the discipline and organisation of a professional army, provokes an existential crisis for Zionist colonialism. Unable to defeat the Palestinian armed resistance in successive battles, Israel has turned instead to intensifying its genocidal violence against unarmed Palestinians as the means to restore its necessary equation of material and ideological force. There are, thus, two logics of war at play in Palestine today: the logic of a war of liberation versus the logic of a colonial war of genocide.

The Disarmed Premise of the Oslo Road

The disarming of the Palestinian national liberation struggle was central to the consolidation of a political framework that could go no further than offering Palestinians at best a quasi-sovereign status, eternally dependent upon the real effective sovereign power of Zionism. While the First Intifada (1987-1993) re-awakened the Palestinian national liberation struggle, and forced the world to again take note of it, the absence of the hard material power of armed struggle left Palestinians with limited leverage in the Oslo 'peace process' that the US and Israel pursued in response to that uprising. In order to be granted recognition as a legitimate political subject and partner in the peace process, the Palestinian Liberation Organisation (PLO) had to permanently renounce armed struggle as a means of pursuing national liberation from Zionist colonialism.[1] Insofar as the Oslo road did not demand a demilitarised and disarmed Israeli partner, the PLO concession on armed struggle amounted to an effective surrender of the material basis of Palestinian sovereignty. Under the Oslo framework, Israel would exclusively hold the monopoly of violence that confers de facto sovereign right,

leaving Palestinian political subjecthood as one which could only operate in so far as it accorded with the aims of Israeli colonial sovereignty. The Palestinian Authority that emerged from Oslo has only been granted recognition as a quasi-sovereign to the extent that it deploys organised violence, not against Zionist colonialism, but rather towards policing Palestinian resistance.[2] The deepening of the colonial equation of force enabled Israel the means to accelerate its theft of Palestinian land, and to impose even greater restraints on Palestinian existence and movement across historic Palestine in the post-Oslo period.

The Oslo framework constituted an attempt to permanently return the Palestinians to the foundational condition of colonialism, the normalisation road wherein the colonial monopoly of violence is assumed to be eternal and irreversible. Upon this road, as Palestinian revolutionary Ghassan Kanafani warned, the Palestinians are forced to exist in a 'world that is not theirs'.[3] It is the Israeli coloniser that holds the material power that ensures that Palestinian life can only ever be ordered against its own flourishing, in service of Israeli colonialism. As across much of the South, however, an "end of history" that took as its premise a permanent colonial and imperial sovereign rule would be undone in Palestine with a return of the resistance road. In the time beyond the "end of history," the renewed challenge to the colonial equation of force has proven to be irreversible, and has now opened a clear road to a liberated Palestine.

Beyond the End of History: The Return of Resistance

"Colonialism is not a thinking machine, nor a body endowed with reasoning faculties. It is violence in its natural state, and it will only yield when confronted with greater violence."
– Frantz Fanon[4]

The contradiction of the colonial equation of force is that it is constantly in dialectical motion with its own negation. From its inception, the colonial imposition of force seeds in the colonised territory an anti-colonial force of resistance. In this unfolding dialectic, the colonial equation seeks to constantly renew itself by imposing an even greater force with the aim of achieving a permanent repression of the anti-colonial negation. The irrepressible contradiction for the coloniser is that the anti-colonial force that re-emerges in response to each round of renewed colonial imposition grows stronger and nearer to its final aim of returning, to recall Fanon, a "greater violence" that alone will make the coloniser yield.

We can see this dynamic unfolding in Israel's invasion and occupation of Lebanon in the 1980s. The logic and tactics of colonial war used to achieve the disarming of the PLO – widespread indiscriminate bombings, siege warfare[5] – would come to constitute the conditions for the re-emergence of the resistance road on even firmer grounds. For it was from the Lebanese Shia communities that bore the brunt of Israel's colonial war alongside the Palestinians[6] that would emerge an armed resistance capable of overturning Israel's equation of force. It bears emphasising here that the Lebanese resistance emerged in alliance with the PLO, and its eventual consolidation as a force capable of defeating Israel cannot be divorced from how it built upon and learnt from the foundations and tactics developed by the Palestinians over the course of their decades long struggle against Zionist colonialism.

Lebanese armed resistance to the Israeli invasion and occupation would come to be consolidated under the leadership of Hizbullah, a Shia Islamist political organisation founded and centred upon the strategic aim of the expulsion of Israel from Lebanon and, even more fundamentally, the ultimate defeat of Israel as a colonial project through the liberation of Palestine[7]. Over a period of two decades, as the Oslo road was being constructed on the basis of an armed Israeli/disarmed Palestinian equation, Hizbullah engaged in a constant refinement and enhancement of its tactics and capabilities for conducting an armed resistance that would

become capable of achieving an equation of force conducive to decolonisation.[8] Such capacities were further enhanced by the strategic depth Hizbullah gained through its role in the development of an emergent regional resistance bloc that included the backing of the Iranian revolutionary state.

By the late 1990s, Hizbullah had acquired the capacity to directly expose the limits of Israeli military power. This included the development and deployment of anti-tank weapons that demonstrated the capacity to transform Israel's hitherto feared hard power capacity to impose force – such as the Merkava tank – into targets for the demonstration of the 'greater violence' of anti-colonial force. In piercing the armour of the Merkavas,[9] Hizbullah not only set in motion the overturning of the material component of the colonial equation of force. Equally crucial here, the material transformation of force generated a further transformation in the ideological or psychological component of force. No longer could Israeli soldiers believe in their own invincibility and thus their capacity to inflict force upon those they occupy with impunity. Henceforth, when Israeli soldiers encountered Hizbullah fighters on the battlefield their increasing psychological disbelief in their armed capacity exposed the weakness of their fighting resolve.[10] From the other direction, the growing strength of Hizbullah's armed capacity served to demonstrate the belief and resolve of its fighters on the battlefield. Combined, the overturning of the material and ideological equation of force would make it impossible for Israel to continue its occupation of Southern Lebanon. In contrast, then, to the Oslo road equation, which allowed Israel to accelerate its theft of Palestinian lands by the turn of the millennium, the resistance road preserved and deepened by Hizbullah expelled Israel from Lebanon and demonstrated to Palestinians how they could construct a sovereign capacity with which to reclaim their lands.

Israel's defeat at the hands of Hizbullah in Southern Lebanon would intensify the crisis of the Oslo paradigm in Palestine and significantly inform the emergence of a post-Oslo trajectory of armed struggle that would ultimately evolve into a rising war of national liberation. In the first instance, Israel's defeat in Southern Lebanon was a devastating blow to its vaunted deterrence capacity which had been central to its ideological projection of an invincible power that could be waged against any form of resistance with impunity. The capacity to stamp out resistance with overwhelming and invincible power is essential to maintaining belief in a Zionist project built upon dispossessing the Indigenous people of Palestine from their lands. Zionists have long recognised that dispossessed Palestinians would never relent in their desire to return to the homes from which they were expelled.[11] Therefore, a powerful deterrence capacity, both in a material and psychological register, was necessary to disincentivise Palestinians from enacting their right to return and to provide Zionist settlers with the belief that they could feel secure living on stolen land. In substantially eroding this deterrence capacity, Hizbullah intensified the existential crisis of Zionist colonialism.

Frustration with the dead end of the Oslo peace process on the one hand, and the evident success of Hizbullah's strategy of armed struggle on the other, converged to significantly shape the emergence and unfolding of the Second Intifada (2000-2005).[12] With the outbreak of the Second Intifada occurring only four months after Israel's expulsion from Southern Lebanon, it was anxious to demonstrate to Palestinians that it still possessed the necessary deterrence capacity, or equation of force, to overwhelmingly suppress Palestinian resistance. It attempted to do so by violently repressing the largely non-violent tactics – e.g. demonstrations, marches - that Palestinians were using in the early stages of the second intifada.[13] However, here the contradiction of the colonial equation of force once again revealed itself, as the more militant Palestinian groups, such as Hamas and Palestinian Islamic Jihad, responded by engaging in armed resistance that would impose greater costs on Israel

for its violent repression of unarmed Palestinian political actions. The shifting of the calculus of the costs of war would compel Israel to abandon its remaining settlements in Gaza, where the costs imposed by armed struggle were most acutely felt. This did not, of course, end the occupation of Gaza, as Israel maintained a control over the territory's land, air, and sea borders which would be ultimately used to impose a devastating blockade. It did, however, powerfully signify, again, how a change in the equation of force was central to the reclamation of Palestinian sovereign rights over their lands.

The 2006 Equation

After expelling Israel from Lebanon in 2000, Hizbullah continued to enhance and develop its military capacities in anticipation of a subsequent war through which Israel would attempt to restore its eroding deterrence capacity. The war arrived in summer 2006, when Israel rejected Hizbullah demands for a prisoner exchange and instead responded by conducting a total war against Lebanon with the expressed intention of eliminating Hizbullah's force capacity. Israel continued to prove incapable of defeating Hizbullah in direct battle during its ground invasion of Lebanon, with Hizbullah fighters, once again, commenting openly on the weak resolve of Israeli fighters they encountered on the battlefield.[14] The continuing reversal of the ideological-psychological component of the equation of force proceeded in step with the material component, with Hizbullah demonstrating a stronger capacity to inflict damage on Israeli military equipment and fire rockets even deeper into Israel.[15] Israel's deterrence capacity was dealt a further blow by not only its failure to achieve its stated aim of eliminating Hizbullah, but even more fundamentally through a further demonstration that the regional resistance was rising in its capacity to permanently overturn Israel's constitutive equation of force.

While Israel suffered a historic, irreversible, defeat in the 2006 summer war, it did, in the course of the conflict, formulate and apply a military doctrine that sought to restore its deterrence capacity through explicitly targeting unarmed civilians for death and civilian infrastructure for destruction in the Dahiya suburb of Beirut.[16] The motive of doing so was to undermine the popular support that sustained Hizbullah's resistance capacity. An Israeli commander articulated the Dahiya doctrine as one in which 'we will wield disproportionate power…and cause immense damage and destruction. From our perspective, these [civilian neighbourhoods] are military bases… harming the population is the only means of restraining Nasrallah'.[17] This doctrine would be applied repeatedly in the subsequent wars Israel periodically unleashed against Gaza over the following two decades.

What we see, then, in the period from 2006 onwards is the capacity of the rising armed resistance to re-open contestation of that which was long assumed to have been settled: the fundamental equation of force underlying Israel's colonial project. In overturning this equation, the armed resistance has opened, irreversibly, the road to liberation and Israel has responded by explicitly returning to its genocidal foundations. The massive death and destruction Israel has routinely visited upon Gaza is not a collateral damage of war; it is the intended outcome of a doctrine that seeks to restore, via the logic of total elimination, an irreversibly eroding deterrence capacity.

The Rising Palestinian War of National Liberation against the Israeli Colonial War of Genocide

The capacity of the Palestinian armed resistance to advance an anti-colonial equation of force was first demonstrated during Israel's 2014 military assault on Gaza. In response to Israel's intensification of its repression in the West Bank in the summer of 2014, and particularly of its imprisonment of hundreds of Palestinians, the armed resistance in Gaza fired rockets into Israel as a signal that such repression would not continue with impunity. Israel sought to repress the armed resistance, and restore the impunity necessary for its survival as a colonial project, by launching a military invasion of

Gaza. It is here, in defence against that invasion, that the Palestinian armed resistance applied the tactics and weaponry that Hizbullah had earlier proven effective in demonstrating to Israel a new equation of force. The Palestinian resistance was able to fire rockets more persistently and deeply into Israel, the impact of which was most notably felt when it disrupted air traffic around Ben Gurion airport.[18] Even more significantly, Palestinian fighters demonstrated the capacity to achieve tactical victories against Israeli military units in direct battle. The new equation of force was demonstrated most powerfully in a direct battle that occurred in the Shuja'iyya refugee camp during Israel's invasion, where the Palestinian resistance deployed guerilla tactics to target and eliminate more than a dozen Israeli soldiers in a single battle.[19] Israel, confronting here evidence of the further deterioration of its deterrence capacity, and incapable of restoring it in direct battle with the Palestinian armed resistance, turned again to its genocidal Dahiya doctrine in an attempt to restore its equation of force.[20] In the night that followed its defeat in battle, Israel launched a wholescale indiscriminate attack on the camp with the express intent of terrorising unarmed civilians and destroying civilian infrastructure.[21] Nearly one hundred civilians were massacred in Israel's brutal attack on Shuja'iyya, and thousands more were killed during the entirety of the 2014 war.[22]

As was the case earlier in Lebanon, the widespread death and destruction imposed by the Dahiya doctrine failed in its objective of eliminating the Palestinian will to resist. On the contrary, the Palestinian resistance proved successful in repelling the Israeli invasion and forcing Israel to agree to terms demanded by the resistance – such as an easing of the blockade – as part of a ceasefire.[23] This emergent challenge to Israel's equation of force was advanced further during the 2021 Unity intifada, where the Gazan armed resistance again directly challenged the impunity with which Israel could engage in land theft in the West Bank and Jerusalem. Rockets were fired from Gaza with the aim of compelling Israel to stop its ethnic cleansing in the Sheikh Jarrah neighbourhood of Jerusalem and its ongoing abuses of worshipers at Al-Aqsa mosque.[24] In responding, again, to Israeli abuses against Palestinians in the West Bank and Jerusalem, the armed resistance in Gaza challenged the division imposed by Israeli colonialism and apartheid in order to weaken and isolate Palestinians. Instead, the 'Sword of Al-Quds' operation provisioned the means for the material unification of Palestinian struggle across the divided zones of occupied Palestine. While Israel attempted to again eliminate the armed resistance in Gaza with airstrikes which killed hundreds of Palestinian civilians, it did not undertake a ground invasion in light of the costs its army suffered during its 2014 invasion. This shifting equation of force would result in an even clearer victory for Hamas, as it imposed costs that forced Israel to end its ethnic cleansing operation in Sheikh Jarrah and its attacks on Al-Aqsa worshippers.[25]

In the two years that followed the Unity Intifada, Israel, having been granted even more diplomatic cover by the Biden administration, proceeded to deepen and accelerate its colonisation of the West Bank. Over this time, hundreds of Palestinians were murdered by the Israeli occupation army.[26] with thousands more being subjected to ethnic cleansing[27] and imprisonment.[28] Affirming the material unification of Palestinian struggle that was advanced during the Unity Intifada, resistance organisations based in Jenin in the West Bank took the lead in conducting armed resistance against Israel's accelerating colonisation. In July 2023, the armed resistance in Jenin repelled an attempted Israeli military incursion into the camp, forcing Israel to retreat without achieving its stated objective of eliminating the Jenin Brigades.[29] The Jenin resistance, in shifting the material equation of force, had the further effect of piercing through the ideological equation that has long granted Israel cover from the 'international community.' In responding to its defeats on the battlefield by returning to its Dahiya doctrine, razing civilian

infrastructure and terrorising the unarmed civilians of Jenin, Israel exposed itself as a state conducting war crimes in service of a project of ethnic cleansing.[30] UN and EU officials, normally quite subservient to Israeli demands, expressed shock and concern regarding Israel's assault on Jenin, openly declaring that this likely constituted a violation of international law.[31]

The victory of the Jenin Brigades this past July gave further strength to the challenge posed by the armed resistance in Gaza to Israel's fundamental equation of force. In the months that followed, Israel would transfer military resources from its Gaza Southern Command to the West Bank in an effort to restore its fading deterrence capacity there.[32] This proved critical to the Al-Aqsa flood operation when it was launched soon thereafter from Gaza.[33] With Israel pre-occupied with monitoring and repressing the armed resistance in the West Bank, Gazan forces were afforded greater cover and room of manoeuver in planning and launching what can, in part, be apprehended as a historic break out of the prison camp like conditions that Israel had imposed on Gaza.[34]

The political demands attached to Al-Aqsa flood emphasise the material unification of the Palestinian national liberation struggle. Al-Aqsa flood was launched with the express purpose of ending Israeli impunity and demanding Israel release Palestinians being held and subject to torture in Israeli prisons, that it end its ethnic cleansing in the West Bank, abuse of worshippers at Al-Aqsa mosque, and an end to the blockade of Gaza.[35] The operation demonstrated a material capacity to permanently and irreversibly overturn the equation of force that underpins Israeli colonial sovereignty. If the logic of Israel's colonial equation of force has been to impose a calculus that disincentivised the dispossessed Palestinians from returning to the lands from which they were expelled in 1948, the anti-colonial equation of force actualises a material basis for a Palestinian sovereign power that can enforce the right of return, reclamation of stolen lands, and an end to the ongoing imprisonment and ethnic cleansing of Palestinians in the West Bank. Al-Aqsa flood, particularly in terms of how rapidly it overwhelmed Israel's southern command, has accelerated the crisis of the ideological component of Israel's equation of force. It is exceedingly difficult to envision how exactly Israeli colonialism can restore its necessary belief in the invincibility of its power to impose itself on Palestinians.

Conceivably, Israel, and its Western backers, could have responded to Al-Aqsa Flood by recognising its political rationality and negotiating a peace settlement on the basis of such recognition. However, in so far as Al-Aqsa Flood expressed a logic of a rising war of national liberation, that was overturning the underlying equation of force, such recognition would amount to a fatal loss of belief in the viability of Israel as a settler colonial project. It is this contradiction that makes the Al-Aqsa Flood operation unintelligible to Israel and the West except as an act of pure irrational savagery that can thus only be responded to with the logic of total elimination. Unable to any longer defeat Palestinians on the battlefield, Israel has turned, finally, to attempting to restore its necessary equation of force with the application of the Dahiya doctrine on an enormous scale. The colonial war of genocide that Israel has launched has as its aim and intended outcome the destruction of the Palestinians as a national people with political claim making capacity. The intentional policy of bombing hospitals, schools, homes, resulting in tens of thousands killed in mere weeks, alongside the intensification of the siege that has starved and dehydrated Palestinians in Gaza, takes as its aim the destruction of the Palestinian will to not only resist, but to reclaim and exercise real effective sovereign power. While the entirety of the Western media and political class has joined Israel in racialising Palestinian violence as an irrational savagery that must be responded to with a war of extermination, the response of the Palestinian resistance has been instructive regarding the longer term horizon. Rather than appeal for its

humanity to be recognised by Western imperialism and Zionist colonialism, the Palestinian resistance has, in continuing to defeat Israel on the battlefield in Gaza, commanded a recognition of its political rationality and thus brought the racialised framework of "irrational savagery" to crisis point. In so doing, it has opened a road beyond the inhumanity of genocidal colonialism that is the foundation of the Western world order.

Bikrum Gill is an assistant professor in the department of political science and core faculty in the ASPECT doctoral program at Virginia Tech. He is the author of the forthcoming book titled 'The Political Ecology of Colonial Capitalism: Race, Nature, and Accumulation'.

References

1   Joseph Massad, 'The "Deal of the Century": The Final Stages of the Oslo Accords' *Al Jazeera Center for Studies*, November 6, 2018.
2   Dianne Buttu, 'The Oslo Agreements – What Happened?' in *From the River to the Sea: Palestine and Israel in the Shadow of 'Peace,'* edited by Mandy Turner (Lexington, 2019), 17-40.
3   Abduljawad Omar and Louis Allday, 'An unyielding will to continue: An interview with Abdaljawad Omar on October 7 and the Palestinian Resistance' *Ebb Magazine*, November 16 2023.
4   Frantz Fanon, *The Wretched of the Earth* (Grove Press, 1963).
5   Rashid Khalidi, 'The Fourth Declaration of War, 1982' in *The Hundred Years War on Palestine: A History of Settler-Colonialism and Resistance, 1917-2017* (Picador, 2020), 140-167.
6   Rashid Khalidi, 'The Fourth Declaration of War, 1982'.
7   Amal Saad-Ghorayeb, *Hizbu'llah: Politics and Religion* (Pluto Press, 2001).
8   David Sousa, 'Three Phases of Resistance: How Hezbollah Pushed Israel out of Lebanon', *E-International Relations*, April 28 2014.
9   David Sousa, 'Three Phases of Resistance: How Hezbollah Pushed Israel out of Lebanon'
10   David Sousa, 'Three Phases of Resistance: How Hezbollah Pushed Israel out of Lebanon'.
11   This realisation was most clearly expressed

by Moshe Dayan in what has been referred to as the 'defining speech of Zionism'. Arguing for the need for the Israeli state to maintain an ever present battle ready posture vis Gaza, Dayan began by noting of the Palestinians: 'Why should we complain of their hatred for us? Eight years have they sat in the refugee camps of Gaza, and seen, with their own eyes, how we have made a homeland of the soil and the villages where they and their forebears once dwelt'. This initial understanding was made, however, for the purpose of warning that the Palestinians will forever long to return home, and that Israel must, thus, always be ready to repel them. Mitch Ginsburg, 'When Moshe Dayan delivered the defining speech of Zionism', *Times of Israel*, 28 April 2016.

12   Bader Araj and Robert J. Brym, 'Opportunity, Culture, and Agency: Influences on Hamas and Fatah Strategic Action during the Second Intifada' *International Sociology*, 25:6, 2010.

13   Bader Araj and Robert J. Brym, 'Opportunity, Culture, and Agency: Influences on Hamas and Fatah Strategic Action during the Second Intifada'.

14   Andrew Exum, 'The Israeli Military Wasn't Ready for This: The notion of an Indomitable Israeli Defence Forces is overdue for a revision', *The Atlantic*, October 2023.

15   Lara Khoury and Seif Da'na, 'Hezbollah's War of Position: The Arab-Islamic Revolutionary Praxis', *The Arab World Geographer*, 12:3-4, 2009.

16   Rashid Khalidi, 'From the Editor: The Dahiya Doctrine, Proportionality, and War Crimes', *Journal of Palestine Studies*, 44:1, 2014.

17   Amos Harel, 'Analysis: IDF Plans to Use Disproportionate Force in Next War', *Haaretz*, 5 October 2008.

18   Jeffrey White, 'The Combat Performance of Hamas in the Gaza War of 2014', *Combating Terrorism Center at West Point*, 7:9, 2014.

19   Jeffrey White, 'The Combat Performance of Hamas in the Gaza War of 2014'.

20   Rashid Khalidi, 'From the Editor: The Dahiya Doctrine, Proportionality, and War Crimes'

21   Mark Perry, 'Why Israel's bombardment of Gaza neighbourhood left US officers stunned', *al-Jazeera*, 2014.

22   Sharif Abdel Kouddous, 'Massacre in She-jaiya', *The Nation*, 2014.

23   Josh Levs, Reza Sayah and Ben Wedeman, 'Israel, Hamas agree to open-ended Gaza truce with core issues left unresolved', *CNN*, August 27 2014.

24   Lina Alsaafin, 'Hamas claims victory as Gaza celebrates ceasefire', *al-Jazeera*, May 21 2021.

25   Lina Alsaafin, 'Hamas claims victory as Gaza celebrates ceasefire'.

26   Awad al-Rujoub, '172 Palestinians killed by Israeli forces in 2023: UN', *Anadolu Ajansi*, August 28 2023.

27   OCHA, 'The other mass displacement: while eyes are on Gaza, settlers advance on West Bank herders', November 1 2023.

28   B'Tselem, 'Statistics on administrative detention in the Occupied Territories', November 20 2023.

29   Dalia Hatuqa, 'Did Israel achieve its goals in Jenin?', *al-Jazeera*, July 6 2023.

30   Dalia Hatuqa, 'Did Israel achieve its goals in Jenin?'.

31   United Nations, 'Israeli air strikes and ground operations in Jenin may constitute war crime: UN experts', July 5 2023 & Agencies, 'EU envoy tours Jenin refugee camp, says IDF operation violated international law', *Times of Israel*, July 8 2023.

32   Yaniv Kubovich and Jonathan Lis, 'Why Israel's Defences Crumbled in Face of Hamas' Assault', *Haaretz*, October 8 2023.

33   Yaniv Kubovich and Jonathan Lis, 'Why Israel's Defences Crumbled in Face of Hamas' Assault'.

34   Tareq Baconi, 'An Inevitable Rupture: Al Aqsa Flood and the End of Partition', *al-Shabaka*, November 26 2023.

35   'Haniyeh outlines the context and objectives of Hamas Operation Al-Aqsa Flood', *MEMO*, October 9 2023.

Israel's War Against Palestinian Culture

Mahmoud Darwish

The following text, edited by Robert K. Beshara, is a transcript of an interview with Mahmoud Darwish taken from the film Palestinian Identity *(dir. Kassem Hawal, 1984), which was made in the aftermath of Israel's invasion of Lebanon in 1982. Israel's recent destruction of educational, archival, and cultural institutions in Gaza must be understood within this broader context: as a deliberate and integral component of Zionism's war against the Palestinian people.*

It seems necessary to me to discern that the Israeli project, concerning itself and the Palestinian people, is not based in its consciousness except on negating the elements of Palestinian existence and of the Palestinian character, whether said elements are on the level of the relationship between the human, the land, history, or memory because the Israeli operation on Palestinian land, since the founding of the Zionist project and to this day, particularly on the ideological level as well as on the level of the political process, has provided us and the foreign observer with nothing but this Israeli conception; the time has come for us all to realise this regarding the future of our political efforts.

As such, the aggression against Palestinian culture is a part of the premeditated and conscious Israeli operation to eradicate the Palestinian character. We are all aware that the purported Israeli claims to Palestinian land result from the formulation of a mythological link between the Israeli people and the Palestinian land. This is why, on the one hand, the arena for the conflict is the ground of existence, which led Zionist consciousness to the inevitability of annihilation because the Palestinian character is the historical negation of the Zionist juridical claims to the land of Palestine. On the other hand, the Israeli existence, which expresses itself as a cultural and civilisational extension of the West, needs to prove to itself firstly and to its supporters in the West secondly that this Palestinian land is barren, not only devoid of population but also of the relationship between the human, the land, and history – i.e., devoid of culture.

We know that the development of Palestinian culture in this trilateral relation of land-human-memory has helped the crystallisation of external awareness as to the legitimacy of the Palestinian right in its conflict with the Zionist assault. Therefore, Palestinian cultural expression became, for Israelis, an immediate danger, for it firstly negates the allegations about the destruction of land by a culturally productive people and secondly because such cultural expression provides a very dangerous testimony as to the anti-cultural operation on whose essence the Zionist presence was founded. Thus, as Palestinian culture expressed the relation of the Palestinian people with their land and their history, the conflict became about confirming this relation and nourishing it on the Palestinian land and abroad as well as reviving the Palestinian memory, as to its history, to such an extent that it penetrated international cultural consciousness. This made Israel resort to dealing with the developing Palestinian culture as an immediate danger to its philosophy, ideology, claims, and rights.

We all know that the condition for Israeli existence is the recognition by the external world of its civilisational superiority over land that it claims was without a people. And if this process is based on an assault against culturally unproductive people, then in the Western conception, it is regarded as a civilising mission.

The development of Palestinian cultural activity compelled Israel to eradicate anything that has to do with a past relation, a present relation, or a future testimony. Consequently, I was not surprised by the Israeli destruction of cultural institutions, for it is a part of the Israeli destruction of the Palestinian homeland, the Palestinian society, and the Palestinian testimony before history because he who steals land does not surprise us by stealing a library. He who kills thousands of innocent civilians does not surprise us by killing paintings. And he who destroys a whole homeland does not surprise us when he destroys a wall on which we hung our paintings. The enemy of the Palestinian tree, the enemy of the Palestinian painting, the enemy of the Palestinian poem is, first and foremost, the enemy of the Palestinian homeland and an enemy of culture, for it is he who combats Palestinian culture.

Mahmoud Darwish (1941-2008), often referred to as Palestine's national poet, was one of the most prominent and celebrated Palestinian intellectuals, poets, and writers of the 20th century.

'Sides Not Solutions': Zionist Propaganda in UK Schools

Alex Turrall

If you are a teacher in the UK then you will already be familiar with the 'Prevent Duty' (or simply, Prevent) and the associated mandatory training that must be refreshed each year. The aim of Prevent, per its statutory guidance, is 'to stop people from becoming terrorists or supporting terrorism.'[1] In the abstract, this policy appears to most educators as an appropriate counterpart to their broader safeguarding duties, with any serious concerns being referred to Channel, a rehabilitation programme. But, in practice its application has been anything but objective. A report by the Muslim Council of Britain (MCB) highlights that Muslims – less than 10% of the UK's population – comprised 60% of Channel referrals. Whereas far-right extremists made up only 10% of Channel referrals, despite 31% of young people 'believing Muslims are taking over England'. This discriminatory bias has led to a two-year-old being referred to social services for singing Allahu Akbar and, presciently, a schoolboy being accused of 'terrorist-like views' for possessing a Boycott, Divestment, Sanctions (BDS) leaflet, with 'Free Palestine' badges being considered extremist. It is worth noting that 80% of Channel referrals were rejected between 2006 and 2013, validating MCB's assessment of Prevent, 'that children are being viewed through the lens of security and practitioners are finding threats where none exist in many cases.'[2]

A general critique of Prevent aside, when completing the training for teachers myself I was curious if the so-called 'Israel-Palestine conflict' would feature. There was nothing particularly prominent, until the 'Promoting Best Practice' section. In its summary, the training listed 'Educate Against Hate' as its sole source of useful classroom resources, and the first on that list is the organisation 'Solutions Not Sides' (SNS).[3] Upon further inspection, I discovered that the SNS training package provides misleading and disingenuous 'both sides' messaging which perniciously supports the legitimacy of Israeli occupation, and that their wider funding and partner network consists of a conspicuous coalition of major Zionist groups.

The Propaganda War on Children

> No one can be in the world, with the world, and with others and maintain a posture of neutrality. I cannot be in the world decontextualised, simply observing life.[4]
> – Paulo Freire

SNS was founded in 2009 by Sharon Booth, former PA to the British Defence Attaché in Jordan, and claims to provide 'a critical approach to education on the Israeli-Palestinian conflict,' offering a wide range of 'teacher guides' and 'student-led learning resources.' There are too many to analyse in full, but an exploration of their key terms, guide to 'conspiracy theories,' and overall message lay bare a disturbing exercise in Zionist propaganda.

The key definitions provided by SNS to supposedly aid its audience's understanding of 'the situation' of Israel's occupation characterise the organisation's broader worldview.[5] They give some historical background to the word 'Apartheid' and note its designation as a 'crime against humanity' by the UN. But nowhere do they mention its application by Israel in Palestine. Painting a both-sides narrative here would of course be folly, since even leading Israeli political figures have categorised it precisely in those terms.[6] Though SNS acknowledge that the Palestinian Boycott, Divestment and Sanctions campaign (BDS) is comparable to 'tactics used to help end Apartheid in South Africa,' they suggest that because some unnamed 'particular individuals' have targeted Jewish rather than Israeli shops, the campaign could be a vehicle for anti-Semitic actions. They also argue that Jews are particularly sensitive to boycotts as they could elicit 'terrible memories and fears for Jewish people' who were subjected to them in Nazi Germany. No mention is made of Israel blocking Palestinian goods, such as in occupied East Jerusalem in 2016,[7] or its 16-year siege of Gaza.[8] Colonialism, we are told, is a system 'of domination, land, economic and population control by one country, power, or empire, over another, in the latter's indigenous land, to the detriment, exploitation, and abuse of the indigenous population.' Although Israel's violent expulsion of 750,000 Palestinians 'undoubtedly required drastic changing of the demographics' (Israel's founding is not labelled colonial),[9] the term colonialism is said to be 'misapplied in the context of modern international agreements, as Israel is now a fully recognised and legitimate state, rather than a temporary foreign power.' While appealing to the authority of international law is plainly fallacious, following a logic that could be applied to all colonial configurations in history, the idea that Israel was not or is no longer a colonial state is also widely disputed, even by Israeli academics.[10] SNS substantiate their claim by stating, despite numerous historical accounts to the contrary,[11] that 'some Israelis are themselves indigenous to the land, as their families have been in the land for many generations.' In fact, as Steven Salaita notes, this is a claim made by Zionists to appropriate the sense of 'access, belonging, biology, culture, jurisdiction, and identity' that true indigeneity connotes.[12] By endorsing these Zionist claims to legitimacy while whitewashing Israel's overtly settler colonial origins, SNS is both explicitly and implicitly defending its historic and continued occupation of Palestine.

On the Holocaust, SNS say that historical comparisons can help contemporary understanding, but 'the occupation of the Palestinian territories is in no way similar to the Holocaust.' It is true that the industrial extermination committed by the Nazis is different to the 75-year process of the Nakba, nevertheless, 'the fate of the Palestinians,' wrote Holocaust survivor Israel Shahak, 'should be discussed *together* with the Holocaust!' If not just for the fact that Nazi expressions like 'thinning out' or 'making clean [of Palestinians]' are common Israeli expressions, Shahak argues that asserting the 'uniqueness' of the Holocaust as a crime solely against Jews not only ignores its other victims, but more importantly, encourages an attitude of indifference and wilful disregard for systematic violations against other human groups in the past, present, or future.[13] And finally, while the Nakba is described as a time of 'utmost devastation for Palestinians,' the SNS material claims that some Israelis associate 'Nakba' with the establishment of Israel (quite correctly, of course), and therefore 'feel upset or threatened by the term.' The implication here is that mentioning the Nakba could elicit emotional responses from both Palestinians and Israelis, and each side should receive equally compassionate treatment regarding those responses. Again, such logic obscures the rationale and motivations behind each of these interpretations, painting each side as equally traumatised, thus obscuring the historical reality of who the perpetrators and victims of the Nakba were. Indeed, it seems fitting that the SNS timeline resource lists Deir Yassin as the sole massacre carried out by Israel,[14] despite it being just one in a long history of such atrocities.[15]

The SNS guide to 'conspiracy theories' deliberately includes some patently ludicrous ideas such as 'Did Jews fake the Holocaust so they could create Israel?' and 'Did Muslims start the Holocaust?' with questions related to some inconvenient truths such as 'Did Israel create ISIS?' SNS claims that this conspiracy theory 'serves to disregard and downplay the active threat that the group [ISIS] continues to advocate for the murder of people in the West and Jewish people.'[16] It is striking that this is their concern given that it is Muslims who constitute the vast majority of terror-related fatalities.[17] But it also belies well-documented Israeli collaboration with like-minded groups such as Jabhat al-Nusra in Syria,[18] as well as Israeli support for ISIS from a geostrategic perspective.[19] Appropriately, for those who want to fact-check any of SNS's claims in this regard, it recommends Bellingcat,[20] a veritable hive of former western military and intelligence officers with a history of spreading disinformation.[21]

The stated purpose of this programme, visualised by a spectrum analogous to horseshoe theory, is to channel any anti-Israel/Palestine conversations, which are considered 'lose-lose,' towards a neutral position, which in reality is a two-state solution. You cannot be pro- one side. No. You should aim to be 'pro-solution,' a wholly nebulous 'winwin' scenario, only achieved through non-violence, and with a single caption: 'Emotions: Hope, empathy, respect, empowerment.'[22] A student-led resource on ultranationalism is particularly pernicious. With big pictures of Milosevic, Stalin, and Hitler[23] it states that 'extreme nationalism promotes the interests of one state or people above all others,'[24] implying to children that support for a single-state solution for Palestine, the establishment of a democratic state for all, and the end of occupation is akin to the ultranationalism of Hitler and an unspeakably heinous proposal.

Since its establishment, SNS has worked with over 400 schools and 60,000 students. But an SNS report of school tours from 2017 is instructive for understanding their actual goals. Despite stating that the 2,079 student participants came from 'a mix of backgrounds,' the report demonstrated a strong focus on areas with proportionally higher Muslim populations (Manchester, Leicester, and two tours of Bradford). In each tour they admit that most students were Muslims, and for the Midlands they even stated that 'to the best of our knowledge, we did not work with any Jewish students during the week.'[25] In fact, in a document entitled 'Solutions Not Sides Business Plan,' which has now been removed from its website, SNS stated that their main targets were 'areas [of Britain] with the largest populations of Jews and/or Muslims.'[26] As this clearly does not square with the majority of students they are engaging with, it is apparent that SNS view Muslim children through the lens of security, and thus provide total continuity with the British government's broader Prevent strategy which disproportionately targets Muslim children.

It is not surprising that an organisation would take the opportunity to occupy a place in the UK's £1.4 billion teacher training market,[27] and doing so would clearly require said organisation's agenda to dovetail with that of British national interests. In the case of Israel, and in the context of 80% of Conservative MPs being members of Israeli lobby group Conservative Friends of Israel,[28] this would mean disseminating information in such a way as to demonstrate tacit support for Israel and affirming 'western values'. In fact, a 2015 SNS donor brochure underscores this well, with members of the 'Occupy' movement 'wearing the Palestinian scarf and raising the Palestinian flag,' being equated with the English Defence League 'raising the Israeli flag.'[29] To be clear, SNS does not deny that it receives funding from the British state, but the following section reveals an organisation that arose within the interests of a profoundly Zionist political milieu.

Solutions Not Sides: Origins

SNS was originally conceived as a flagship school programme by OneVoice Europe (OVE).[30] OneVoice (with branch names OneVoice International, OneVoice Israel, and OneVoice Palestine) was founded in 2002 by billionaire Daniel Lubetzky. Its stated aim is focusing on leveraging a critical but largely untapped resource within the Israeli and Palestinian public: the centrist mainstream who support resolution of the conflict through a negotiated and mutually-acceptable two-state solution.'[31] It is worth noting that Lubetzky sits on the advisory council for the Zionist lobby group, Israel Policy Forum,[32] and is a director of the Anti-Defamation League (ADL),[33] a long-time collaborator with American imperialism in the suppression of social movements.[34]

OneVoice previously had on its board 'State Department Special Advisor Dennis Ross, former Israeli Deputy Defence Minister Efraim Sneh, and former Israeli military ruler of the occupied West Bank General Danny Rothschild.'[35] This has now changed but for a convoluted, but later revealing, reason. From 2013-2014, the United States funded OneVoice Israel (OVI) and OneVoice Palestine (OVP) with over $300k in the run up to the 2015 Israeli elections.[36] OVI then merged with V15, a new 'grassroots' group advised by Barack Obama's former national field advisor Jeremy Bird.[37] V15 then merged with OVI and they were both subsequently absorbed by a new organisation, Darkenu (Our Path).[38]

Darkenu was founded in 2016 by former executive director of OVI, Polly Bronstein,[39] with the help of former IDF General and Deputy Minister of Defence, Ephraim Sneh, and former IDF pilot and now businessman, Kobi Richter.[40] Darkenu and Commanders for Israel's Security organised the annual 'Rabin Rally' in 2017, inviting six former IDF chiefs of staff,[41] and boasting speakers such as former Mossad chief, Shabtai Shavit,[42] and retired Major General, Amnon Reshef.[43] In-

deed, One Voice International still exists as a separate entity, and has provided funding to the tune of $15 million since 2015 for its two major partners in Israel and Palestine, Darkenu and Zimam respectively.[44] Darkenu's current board members include former Brigadier General of the infamous Golani Brigade (who recently carved the Star of David into a park in Gaza),[45] Baruch Spiegel, former paratrooper Yizhar Shai, and original founder of the One Voice Movement in Israel, Assaf Halachmi. Its stated mission is to 'organise, amplify, and empower the moderate majority of Israelis, both Jewish and Arab, to exert influence on government policy and on the public discourse, ensuring our nation acts in line with … the spirit of Zionism.'[46]

The so-called non-partisanship at the heart of Darkenu's mission is clearly non-existent, but how does this relate to SNS? On its current webpage, SNS emphatically reject the claim that it is funded by OneVoice: 'SNS has received no funding from OneVoice since becoming an independent charity [in 2019], and even prior to that, all SNS funding was separately raised and held as restricted funds.'[47] SNS received £90k of 'net assets from OneVoice Europe' according to their 2020 financial statement.[48]

Interestingly, the Wayback Machine internet archive shows that the FAQ section for SNS, and the question of OneVoice funding, was added after November 2nd, 2023. Their FAQs were previously listed elsewhere. Their statement on funding also specifies that they do not 'share an office' with OneVoice. It seems likely that the page was updated following a viral tweet from activist and rapper Lowkey (Kareem Dennis) on November 17th, who suggested that they share an office on Primrose Hill.[49] Similarly, in response to an FAQ about funding by the British state, the 2022 SNS website stated that they do not 'receive funding from the government of any other country or from individuals or organisations in any other country – all its funding for its work in the UK is from British sources.' This has now been removed and replaced with a vague assertion that 'other SNS funding comes mainly from grants by trusts and foundations and contributions from schools.'

Per financial reports from 2016 to 2021, with the stated aim of ensuring 'that young people are more aware of the nuances behind the conflict in Israel and Palestine,'[50] the British government granted SNS £350k.[51] SNS funding from the British government is not in question, and they admit as much on their website, though they caveat that 'there has never been any governmental input or interference.' But why would they have to interfere if SNS is providing the same 'balanced' view of Israeli occupation as the British state?

Among its list of partners, SNS has received £120k from the Alan and Babette Sainsbury Charitable Fund, which lists former Conservative MP and President of the Conservative Friends of Israel (1997-2005) Timothy Sainsbury as a trustee.[52] SNS also received £310k between 2018 and 2021 from the Pears Foundation.[53] The Pears Foundation, in collaboration with Britain and Israel, provided £1.4m to establish the Britain Israel Research and Academic Exchange Partnership (BIRAX), a project specifically designed to undermine calls for an academic boycott of Israel in British universities. Its executive chair, Trevor Pears, sat on the board of the Conservative Friends of Israel and major Israel lobby group, BICOM.[54]

Given the litany of Zionist financial backers, it is odd that SNS categorically deny such a relationship with OneVoice. In fact, the notable absence of OneVoice in their list of partners twinned with such a strong 'separation' statement implies the relationship is no longer active. This begs the question as to why SNS still list Darkenu, a later evolution of OneVoice Israel, as a key partner, and one whom they use to platform Israeli speakers in British schools?

Sides Not Solutions

From 'Solutions Not Sides' course materials to its origins and partnerships, it is evident that, contrary to the name, it has firmly chosen a side. With the support of the British state, it is enacting an insidious propaganda campaign to subtly deceive children and educators across the UK.

By presenting Palestinian and Israeli needs as equally understandable and valid, SNS has sacrificed pedagogical integrity at the altar of spurious 'impartiality,' and its covert promotion of a two-state solution is essentially campaigning for the continuation of Israeli occupation, and with it the daily brutality meted out against the Palestinians.

As Paulo Freire warns, the promise of neutrality in education should be a red flag for all critically conscious parents and educators, for 'Washing one's hands of the conflict between the powerful and the powerless means to side with the powerful, not to be neutral.'[55]

Alex Turrall is an independent researcher and primary school teacher. The author wants to thank Louis Allday for his thoughtful feedback when writing this piece, and his consistently principled conduct which continues to guide them. It is an honour to be included in this collection.

References

1   Home Office, 'Prevent duty guidance: for England and Wales', 2023.
2   Muslim Council of Britain, 'Meeting Between David Anderson QC and the MCB: Concerns on Prevent', 2015.
3   Educate Against Hate, 'Teachers Classroom Resources', 2023.
4   Paulo Freire, *Pedagogy of Freedom: Ethics, Democracy, and Civic Courage, trans. Patrick Clarke* (Rowman & Littlefield, 2001), 73.
5   Solutions Not Sides, 'A Guide to Vocabulary on the Topic of Israel-Palestine', 2023.
6   Chris McGreal, 'Amnesty says Israel is an apartheid state. Many Israeli politicians agree' (*The Guardian*, 2022.
7   Rania Zabaneh, 'Israeli ban on Palestinian goods in Jerusalem slammed', *Al Jazeera*, 2016.
8   Tamara Nassar, 'Israel cuts fuel, Gaza goes dark', *The Electronic Intifada*, 2020.
9   From its inception, Zionism has been an avowedly colonial project. In his 1925 essay

The Iron Wall, key Zionist founder, Vladimir Jabotinsky, wrote that 'Zionism is a colonisation adventure.' In a July 2023 speech, current Israeli President, Benjamin Netanyahu, remarked that 'One hundred years after the "iron wall" was stamped in Jabotinsky's writings we are continuing to successfully implement these principles.' Additionally, the first Zionist bank was named the 'Jewish Colonial Trust' and the entire campaign was supported by the 'Palestine Jewish Colonisation Association' and the 'Jewish Agency Colonisation Department'. See Decolonise Palestine, 'Zionism is not colonialism, just Jewish self-determination', 2023; and Prime Minister's Office (Israel), 'Excerpt from PM Netanyahu 's Remarks at the State Memorial Ceremony for Ze'ev Jabotinsky', 2023.

10   Ilan Pappé. 'Shtetl Colonialism: First and Last Impressions of Indigeneity by Colonised Colonisers', *Settler Colonial Studies*, 2:1, 39-58.

11   Many academic books dispute Zionist claims to an ancestral as mythological. See Eyal Weizman, *Hollow Land: Israel's Architecture of Occupation* (Verso, 2012); Shlomo Sand, *The Invention of the Land of Israel: From Holy Land to Homeland, trans. Geremy Forman* (Verso, 2012); and Shlomo Sand, *The Invention of Jewish People*, trans. Yael Lothan (Verso, 2009).

12   Steven Salaita. 'Inter/Nationalism from the Holy Land to the New World: Encountering Palestine in American Indian Studies', *Native American and Indigenous Studies*, 1(2), 133.

13   Israel Shahak, '"The Life of Death": An Exchange', *The New York Review of Books*, 1987.

14   Solutions Not Sides, 'A Timeline of Events in Palestine-Israel', 2023.

15   Palestine Remix, 'Timeline of Palestine's History', 2023.

16   Solutions Not Sides, 'A Guide to Conspiracy Theories Around the Topic of Israel-Palestine', 2023.

17   National Counterterrorism Center, '2011 Report on Terrorism', 14.

18   Patrick Donovan Higgins, 'Gunning for Damascus: The US War on the Syrian Arab Republic', *Middle East Critique*, 32:2, 234

19   Efraim Inbar, *ISIS: The Dangers for Israel* (Begin-Sadat Centre for Strategic Studies, 2016), 16.

20   Solutions Not Sides, 'Fact Checker Resource Post', 2023.

21   Alan Macleod, 'How Bellingcat Launders National Security State Talking Points into the Press', *Mintpress News*, 2021.

22   Solutions Not Sides, 'How to Tackle Anti-Jewish & Anti-Muslim Bullying Around the Issue of Israel-Palestine, 2023.

23   The conflation of Stalin and Hitler is in itself a misleading comparison. See Domenico Losurdo, 'Stalin and Hitler: Twin Brothers or Mortal Enemies?', trans. Frank Ruda, *Crisis and Critique, 2016*, Vol. 3, No. 1. pp. 32-47.

24   Solutions Not Sides, 'Nationalism: Israeli and Palestinian Narratives and Symbols', 9.

25   Solutions Not Sides, 'Spring Term 2017 Report – Regions: Bradford, Manchester, East Midlands, and Bradford', 2017.

26   Ben White, 'When it comes to Palestine, 'taking sides' and 'solutions' are not mutually exclusive', 2018.

27   Jens Van den Brandle and James Zuccollo, 'The cost of high-quality professional development for teachers in England', *Education Policy Institute*, 2021, 12.

28   James Hughes, 'Why did London School of Economics censor this article on Israel's lobby?', *The Electronic Intifada*, 2023.

29   It is, of course, revealing that an organisation which prides itself on being sensitive to cultural references would sincerely refer to the keffiyeh, a traditional Palestinian head-dress, as simply a scarf. See Solutions Not Sides, 'Information for Donors', 2015.

30   This fact is stated by OneVoice Europe Board member Katellin Teller in her 2023 PhD thesis and is corroborated by financial statements from OneVoice Europe. See Katelin Teller (2023). 'Organisational Learning, Politics and Change: The Mundane and the Extraordinary in Peacebuilding. A case study of OneVoice (US), Darkenu (Israel), Zimam (Palestine) and Solutions Not Sides (SNS) (UK)', PhD thesis The Open University, 93; and OneVoice Europe, 'Unaudited Trustees Report and Financial Statements for the Year Ended 31 March 2016', (Charity Commission, 2016), 9.

31   OneVoice Movement, 'Our History', 2023.

32   Israel Policy Forum, 'Board of Directors', 2023.

33   ADL, 'Our Board of Directors: Daniel

Lubetzky', 2023.

34   Drop the ADL, 'The ADL is not an ally: A Primer', 2023.

35   Ali Abunimah, 'One Voice: manufacturing consent for Israeli apartheid', *The Electronic Intifada*, 2009.

36   United States Senate Committee on Homeland Security and Governmental Affairs, 'Review of U.S. State Department Grants to OneVoice', 2015.

37   Julie Hirschfeld Davis, 'Former Obama Campaign Aide Now Works to Oust Netanyahu', *The New York Times*, 2015.

38   Katelin Teller (2023). 'Organisational Learning, Politics and Change: The Mundane and the Extraordinary in Peacebuilding. A case study of OneVoice (US), Darkenu (Israel), Zimam (Palestine) and Solutions Not Sides (SNS) (UK)', PhD thesis The Open University, 90.

39   PR Newswire, 'OneVoice Israel Partners with V15 to Change Status Quo', 2015.

40   Pamela Peled, 'We'll do it our way', (The Jerusalem Post, 2016).

41   Andrew Tobin, 'Leftists say Rabin commemoration 'whitewashes' assassination', *The Times of Israel*, 2017.

42   Jacob Magid and Times of Israel Staff, '85,000 attend rally marking 22nd anniversary of Rabin's murder', *The Times of Israel*, 2017.

43   Gideon Levy, 'Yitzhak Rabin Memorial 2017: War Is Over if You Want It - Just Don't Mention the Occupation', *Haaretz*, 2017.

44   OneVoice, 'Impact Report: Get to Know OneVoice', 2022.

45   Michael Horovitz, 'Honouring fallen, Golani troops trace giant Star of David into captured terror outpost', *The Times of Israel*, 2023.

46   Darkenu, 'Who Are We? Vision', 2023.

47   Solutions Not Sides, 'FAQs about SNS' work, mission and goals', 2023.

48   Solutions Not Sides, 'Report and financial statements for the year ended 31 August 2020', (Charity Commission, 2020), 9.

49   It is not clear when exactly it was updated as, at the time of writing, the Wayback archive had not captured a snapshot of the website since November 2nd, 2023.

50   Ministry of Housing, Communities & Local Government, 'Annual Report and Accounts: 2019-20', 364.

51   It is telling that the government's 2018 'Action Against Hate' report and their 2018 annual report actually confuse SNS with OneVoice. See Home Office, 'Action Against Hate The UK Government's plan for tackling hate crime: 2018 – two years on', 11; and Ministry of Housing, Communities & Local Government, 'Annual Report and Accounts: 2018-19', 139.

52   Giving is Great, 'Alan & Babette Sainsbury Charitable Fund: Grants Made', 2023.

53   Giving is Great, 'Solutions Not Sides: Donations from Grant Makers', 2023.

54   Hilary Aked, 'Billionaire donor using British Council to combat Israel boycott', *The Electronic Intifada*, 2016.

55   Paulo Freire, *The Politics of Education: Culture, Power, and Liberation*, trans. Donaldo Macedo (Bergin & Garvey, 1985), 122.

An Interview with Amal Saad on Hizbullah and the Northern Front

The following is an abridged transcript of an interview held on November 11th for an episode of The East is a Podcast *guest-hosted by Louis Allday.*

Louis Allday: Hello everyone. Welcome to the *East is a Podcast*. I'm a guest host today. Longtime friend of the show, my name's Louis Allday. I'm an author and historian and I'm very happy to be speaking to one of the pre-eminent experts in the world on Hizbullah, Amal Saad, who is a lecturer in politics and IR at Cardiff University. She's written one of the best, seminal books on the party and is currently working on another, and at this juncture, for obvious reasons it's great that we can get her thoughts on both the latest speech of Hizbullah's Secretary General, Sayyid Hassan Nasrallah, earlier today, and also a general analysis of the party and its position in the ongoing situation. So welcome, Amal. Thank you very much.

Amal Saad: Hey Louis, thanks for having me on. It's great to have a chance to talk in more depth about what's going on and about Hizbullah specifically. I don't usually get a chance to do that in mainstream media, so thanks for having me.

LA: Exactly. And hopefully we can go a bit beyond the short sound bites that you're often forced into in the mainstream media. So, as we speak right now, on November the 11th, Nasrallah finished his latest speech, not long ago. As always, and perhaps at the current moment now more than ever before, because of the unique nature and role of Hizbullah both nationally, regionally, and globally now, Nasrallah is often forced to address a number of different audiences simultaneously in his speeches. Even today, I was struck actually that he – this is a less common one – he addressed people in the West when he mentioned the importance of protests there. So, could we maybe start by talking through what you think were the main messages of his speech today to those different and overlapping audiences?

AS: Yeah. I think first of all, it's important to note that today's speech wasn't really one meant for consumption outside of Hizbullah's constituency, because the occasion was Martyr's Day and Nasrallah makes this speech every single year, and it's usually aimed at a domestic audience, though sometimes he'll have messages for Israel, and by domestic I also obviously mean Palestine and the Muslim and Arab world as well. So, I think this speech wasn't the same as the last speech he made [on November 3rd], the long awaited one where there was no occasion for that, no religious or political or any other occasion, that was just to respond to events.

So, if Martyr's Day hadn't been commemorated, he would not have made a speech today. Because he didn't actually add anything new, I think in terms of addressing Israel or the US. It was mainly just to give a roundup of what's been going on since his last speech, and what the different actors have contributed since then which he did, quite extensively. But I think the main message in terms of the sort of local Lebanese, Palestinian, wider Arab and Muslim audience was the idea that Israel's aim behind the genocide of Palestinians isn't just revenge, and is in fact quite strategic. And the aim is to get Palestinians and Lebanese and everyone else to submit, to surrender. To implant a sense of despair and defeat. And this actually goes back to a recurring theme which goes back to a much earlier speech that he made in 2008, which was about the battle of awareness or battle of consciousness. And that speech was made in the aftermath of [Imad] Mughniyeh's assassination. And it actually focused a lot on how Israel was from day one, like from the very first invasion, even before 1982, like in '78, was constantly trying to what he calls 'expunge' this resistance awareness from people's hearts and minds and that the biggest challenge was to get people initially to view it as [not] unrealistic or irrational to resist or fight Israel, and how that had to be overcome. And then later on it became a question of can Israel be defeated? And it could, in 2006 we saw that. And then the last phase being can Palestinians and Lebanese and Muslims generally, can they bring about the downfall of the Zionist regime, and that too, in Nasrallah's opinion is something feasible and realistic. So, this is the sort of battle we're talking about. It's not just one of hearts and minds like in counter insurgency, it's different.

So, in that speech, Nasrallah focused a lot on the importance of awareness and political consciousness and how this psychological element was a major part of the battle. So, it transcends the military aspects and obviously that's a very important aspect, but the psychological and emotional aspects were as important. So, this is a recurring theme and it's one that Nasrallah

has touched upon in many other speeches, in fact, not just the one today. As for the other messages you were asking, yes, he did address the protests, throughout Europe and the US and the Western world. But as I said, most of it was actually geared towards a more local audience.

LA: It's related to what you were saying, but to zoom out slightly from the specifics of the speech today, I was wondering if you could talk a little bit about the relationship between Hizbullah and the Palestinian factions, because I think probably a fair number of people are not fully aware of the history and the depth of that relationship, and specifically the fact that it – and this was alluded to in what you were saying a minute ago – it transcends some kind of quid pro quo transactional relationship and is actually something lot more than that.

AS: That's right. I think the first thing we have to look at is that Hizbullah was born out of an Israeli invasion. So its raison d'être is Israeli invasion, which is intricately tied, you know Israel's existence is tied to the Palestinians being dispossessed of their homeland. So, the two are very tightly interwoven from its very birth.

And of course, in Hizbullah's ideology, there's the religious legal obligation that Hizbullah has as a body of believers, and their mission is to liberate Palestine, all of historic Palestine, to be very precise, not just the [post-1967] occupied territories, not just parts of Lebanon that remain occupied. So this is an ideological tenet for Hizbullah. It's not just strategic or emotional or just political. It's a very deep ideology. And Hizbullah is a very ideological, religiously ideological, organisation as you know so I think it's always important to refer back to that as well.

In terms of the relationship historically speaking there's a very long history of military cooperation between Hizbullah and not just Hamas and Islamic Jihad who emerged after the mid-eighties, but even before that with Fatah. So the relationship with the Palestinians goes way back. And even before the birth of Hamas and Islamic Jihad, as early as the early 1980s before Hizbullah was even officially born in '82, the groups that later merged and became, this umbrella group called Hizbullah, fought alongside Palestinians.

In fact, many Hizbullah members once fought with Fatah. For example, you have Hajj Imad Mughniyeh, [Mustafa] Badreddine both of them were part of Fatah's Elite Force 17, for example. So from very early on, from the Israeli invasion in '82 there were joint operations. As I said, before Hizbullah was officially born as an organisation. And then after they liberated Beirut in the mid-eighties they worked with other factions before the birth of Hamas and Islamic Jihad. They trained Fatah. And what a lot of people forget is that Hizbullah fought the Amal movement during the War of the Camps between 1985 and 1988. And that was in support of the PLO and the Palestinians. So there was the Amal movement and behind it, the Syrian state. So, Hizbullah was effectively fighting Amal and Syria in support of the PLO. So that's something that is often forgotten, this very long-standing history.

And even after the Oslo Accords, Hizbullah didn't cut off ties with Fatah. They continued to work closely with the organisation from 2000 to 2006. Apparently, they would follow a lot of their operations down to minute details and coordinate with all the factions. We're talking here about al-Aqsa Martyrs Brigades, so not just Hamas and Islamic Jihad or the PFLP. So this was all despite Oslo. And then there are certain events as well. For example, the Karine-A Affair in 2002. If you recall, when Israel seized a Palestinian Authority owned ship that was loaded, I think with 50 tons of weapons that were sent from Iran and involved Hizbullah. It was seized in 2002, and had Iran and Hizbullah's fingerprints all over it.

And then of course you had the 2008 arrest of Sami Shihab who was a Hizbullah operative, and he was arrested in Egypt. And he was accused of smuggling weapons into Gaza. He was trying to infiltrate Gaza from Egypt. And I recall Nasrallah saying then that he was proud and he wasn't going to hide the fact that Hizbullah was indeed trying to help arm Hamas. So there are these well-known facts that are documented. Obviously, there are also Hamas officials in Lebanon, including Saleh al-Arouri who left Qatar in 2017, as well as other Hamas officials. You've also got the head of Islamic Jihad, Ziyad al-Nakhalah, in Beirut.

One more thing I forgot to mention [is] the prisoner exchanges, like in 2004, Hizbullah traded in the bodies of three IDF soldiers for 30 Lebanese and 400 Palestinians. It traded them with Israel. And then again in 2008, in return for two dead Israeli soldiers, Hizbullah succeeded in releasing not just Samir al-Qantar and four other Hizbullah fighters, but also the bodies of 199 Palestinian, Lebanese and Arab fighters.

So that's also further evidence of support Hizbullah has given the Palestinians, and that's not to mention more military, more detailed military cooperation. For example, the bunkers that Hamas built, this network of tunnels that was traced back to, you know, we saw Hamas' performance in 2008-2009 in that war, when Israel invaded Gaza, that's when we first noted the tunnels and it was very clear then that they had the fingerprints of Imad Mughniyeh all over it as well, because Hizbullah's tunnels were also exposed in 2006.

LA: In addition to those decades long logistical, military and political relations could you just say something briefly about how the relationship is not solely some kind of logistical political alliance and actually speaks to something deeper in the connection?

AS: The term Resistance Axis, when we talk about this alliance between Hizbullah, Iran,

Syria, [the] Palestinian resistance factions, the PMU in Iraq, and Yemen's Ansar Allah or just to call it Yemen now, it's easier. It's called the Resistance Axis because it was formed on the basis of resisting Israel. Many people say Iran is the backbone of this alliance. That's true in the sense that it gives all the material support because it's the strongest power in this alliance. But what gives it its ideological backbone, I would say, is the Palestinian factions. Because of the sanctity of Palestine, not just religious sanctity, but political sanctity as well. And we're not just talking here about the al-Asqa Mosque or Jerusalem, we're talking about the Palestinian cause generally. Without the Palestinian cause, I don't think the Resistance Axis would be called the Resistance Axis to begin with.

And Hizbullah emerged, as I said, as a response to [the] Israeli invasion and occupation of Lebanon. But Hizbullah has never tied its arms solely to the liberation of Lebanese territory. It's always insisted that even if Israel withdraws from all Lebanese territory – which it has yet to do – but even if it did, the very existence of Israel, as Hizbullah puts it, as an aggressive entity, an expansionist aggressive entity, necessitates that Hizbullah needs to remain armed to support Palestinians in their quest to liberate their territory. So this in fact goes beyond ideology. It's related to the very identity of Hizbullah, its political identity as a resistance actor. And so I think even if its relations sour with Hamas, which they have [previously] by the way, they have soured, during the period of Hizbullah's intervention in Syria and the war in Syria ties with Hamas... There was a rupture, I wouldn't say severance of ties completely, not with Hizbullah anyway, or with Iran, but there was a freezing of ties, if you like. And they deteriorated, but they were never fully cut off. There was some element of assistance which remained, I don't know the extent of it. There were different reports from different people and different

sources, but it never officially ended. So, despite the deterioration, and many people thought that, that relationship could never be repaired, they were wrong because again, because of the sanctity of this relationship, and it could transcend Hamas and has, in fact, because you have other groups on the ground, it's not just tied to Hamas specifically.

LA: Something that comes to mind as you're saying that is something that happened in 2001, which I know you are aware of, but not everyone listening may be, is that after 9/11 the US offered Hizbullah better relations and removal from all US terror lists if it ended its support for the Palestinians and severed all ties with Hamas, Islamic Jihad and with Syria as well. Nasrallah and Hizbullah obviously refused this offer. And when he was asked about his response and their refusal, Nasrallah said that to have done that would've been 'a total elimination of Hizbullah's heart and head.' So it speaks to the centrality of those connections and of that cause.

Moving away from the kind of ideological and I'm not sure if emotional is the right word, but this kind of sanctity, the sanctity of that connection – notwithstanding the depth and the sincerity of Hizbullah's support for the Palestinian factions and the cause generally, something that you've pointed out recently, which I think is also illuminating and important, is that it's not simply a question of altruism because from their perspective, it is also in the Lebanese national interest to act in this way. And I think that is something that is true of all the various members of the Axis Resistance in a kind of inter-connected way. And I think, people in bad faith have often argued that means they're using the Palestinian cause or the factions in a very cynical way. But I think as we are discussing that that's not true, and there's a whole other kind of perspective, but that doesn't mean they're acting solely out of altruism. So could you talk a little bit more about the perceived national interest in Lebanon of Hizbullah to continue this position, but then also how that inter-connects with the other members of the access resistance.

AS: So first of all, yes, there is a huge part that is moral, ideological, emotional, the various aspects. And that's the solidarity military campaign that Hizbullah is waging now in support of the Palestinians and that's prompted by all those things. But on the other hand, you also have the national security motivation, national security interests, at least how Hizbullah defines them and Nasrallah has actually on several occasions talked about this being in relation to Lebanon's national interest as well, and that we can't, again, another very sort of long standing theme, we can't extricate – because many Lebanese people who oppose, Hizbullah and its resistance say 'it's not in our interests. You're acting against Lebanon's interests,' and they want to neutralise Lebanon and that's always been a very absurd notion for Hizbullah because they don't see this as something you can extricate from whether you want to or not, you can't extricate events in Lebanon from Palestine. So they've always argued that protecting the southern front, which is Israel's northern front, is a strategy of self-defence, of national interest. And I call this anticipatory self-defence. It's not the same as pre-emptive. A lot of people confuse the two because, pre-emptive, you don't need an actual threat or an imminent threat. Whereas with anticipatory self-defence, there has to be an imminent threat. And obviously pre-emptive is linked to pre-emptive war, [which] was linked to Bush's 'War on Terror'. So it's a completely different concept... anticipatory self-defence, because Israel has a track record of invading Lebanon, of annexing Lebanon and regards Lebanon as part of Eretz Israel, Greater Israel.

LA: And it continues to occupy a portion of Lebanese territory.

AS: Exactly. And we saw this Israeli military official just the other day saying Lebanon is part of Eretz Israel, just like Gaza is. So they haven't given up this dream, and I don't think they ever will, until they're finally defeated. So Hizbullah believes that it should engage in anticipatory self-defence to prevent a pre-emptive attack [on Lebanon] from Israel. And in fact, this has been stated by several Israeli officials recently, one of whom is Yoav Gallant, the Israeli Defence Minister. He's been calling for pre-emptive strikes on Lebanon and trying to persuade Netanyahu of this and other officials have as well. And so the idea here is that anticipatory warfare would prevent such an attack. And there's also this speech by the Iranian Foreign Minister, [Hossein] Amir-Abdollahian, he said last month and he quoted Nasrallah, and I'm just going to read the quote he said: 'Mr Nasrallah also said that if we don't take immediate action, we will have to fight with the Zionist forces in Beirut tomorrow.' Meaning if we don't fight them today in Gaza, in occupied Palestine rather, then we're going to have to fight them in Beirut. So again, here, this is the idea of anticipatory self-defence.

So this is the main idea behind the national security interest. And I think all actors in the Resistance Axis also have this idea of, or strategic vision, to protect their security interests. In fact, the US has in the past not just tried to persuade Hizbullah to relinquish the Palestinian cause, it's done the same with Iran in 2003 with the 'Grand Bargain.' It's done the same with Syria with a list of demands, again, in 2003, it was after the Iraq invasion really. They tried to scare different actors who were supporting Palestine. Tried to scare them, tried to blackmail them or offer carrots and sticks in exchange for giving up the Palestinian cause and giving up support to Palestinian groups. And they haven't, not just out of ideological reasons, but also because they do not see this as serving their national security interests.

LA: Thank you. Related to the regional dimension, how do you see the kind of standing and popularity of Hizbullah currently? And I guess by that I mean both on a popular and state level as well, because there are those, I think some, as we mentioned before we started recording, whose criticism is in bad faith, but I think there are some people who publicly or otherwise have a feeling that Hizbullah is 'not doing enough.' What would you say to that position?

AS: Well, I think it's very natural for people to feel very frustrated, and especially Palestinians in particular who are besieged, not just by Israel, by the entire world. Because Hizbullah is seen as much more powerful than Hamas, there is this sense that Hizbullah, if it did want to, could take on Israel. There are two main problems with this. The first being that this is a very emotional response and there's nothing wrong with that in and of itself, but in order to really understand where Hizbullah stands in this and why it's not choosing to intervene [more] immediately. First of all, we've got to look at Nasrallah's speech. Nasrallah has in the past never actually announced Hizbullah's military strategy before embarking on one. So that doesn't mean Hizbullah isn't going to intervene, by the way, just because last time [November 3rd] and today he didn't make the same kind of announcement he did in 2006, which was, look out of your window. Watch that [Israeli] ship, watch that warship burn. First of all, he didn't say it before it burned, did he? He said it after it was burning or as it was burning. And he said this today: you can't start with the speech and the announcement and then from there wait for things to develop on the battlefield.

LA: He said eyes should be on the battlefield and things will be announced after not be-

fore.

AS: Exactly, and that's what happened. In fact, in 2006, he did not make that announcement before Hizbullah launched anti-ship missiles. That's not what happened. So we have yet to see if Hizbullah will find the need to fully intervene, and we can discuss that in a minute. In terms of Hizbullah's overall strategy, in terms of intervening or not, I recall these questions were asked well before Twitter became a thing. It was late 2008, early 2009. The same questions were asked, is Hizbullah going to intervene and help Hamas in Gaza? There was an [Israeli] invasion then too. It's the same rationale or logic. And that is, first of all, Hizbullah is not a populist movement. Nasrallah is not a populist leader. Hizbullah is responsive, it responds to Israel's military actions, but it's not reactive and it doesn't have an emotional mind, but a strategic and pragmatic mind. It's very horrible to say this, but unfortunately no matter what the casualty toll is, that doesn't just apply to Gaza, but also to Lebanon. No matter how high the casualty toll and Hizbullah was reprimanded by many Lebanese back in 2006… they blamed Hizbullah for the destruction and deaths that Israel inflicted on Lebanon. But again, these decisions are not dictated by casualty tolls. So there's no certain number of civilians who have to be martyred for Hizbullah to intervene. I think this has become something much clearer now. That the strategy has to be one which responds to objectives and Hamas has laid out objectives. And more important than anything, I think for Hizbullah is to see Hamas survive.

I think that this idea that if Hizbullah would intervene immediately, this would put an end to the bloodshed. It's not very realistic to be honest. And if anything, Hizbullah's intervention, I mean it's already intervening obviously, but I mean in a much bigger way, Hizbullah's, waging an all-out war, right? This is what people are talking about. That would not just open a second front. That would open many fronts because in fact, Nasrallah has said in the past that the next time there's a war on Lebanon, it won't just be Hizbullah, it's going to be tens of thousands, and he even added even hundreds of thousands of fighters, from across the Resistance Axis. So it would also entail that these other fronts, which are not fully open yet, be they from the Iraqi PMU, Syria, Yemen, they would all open much more fully. And so we are talking here not just about the opening of a Lebanese front, we're talking not just about a regional conflict, but an international conflict potentially as well, because there's also the fact that there's the US there. And so if Hizbullah intervenes in a bigger way, it's not just confronting Israel, it's going to be confronting the US as much, if not more. And Nasrallah has in fact threatened this. The US only a few days ago deployed a nuclear submarine for God's sake. So we're not dealing here just with Israel, Israel's but a proxy in this. The US is the real, major power behind this. And it's for the first time in Israel's history [the US] has come to its aid, direct aid, not just with billions of dollars, but with arms and with a thousand – they're not many, but who knows if they'll increase – with a thousand troops with elite commandos, and so on. So we're talking here about an international conflict, not just a regional one that would lead to many more deaths. That would be devastating.

And yes, Hizbullah could bring life in Israel to a standstill. It could mutually assured destruction from both sides. But that means also destruction in Lebanon and also potentially destruction in other places too, by other participants. So it's not really that simple. It wouldn't necessarily end the war. It would probably prolong it, and I think that perhaps from Hizbullah's perspective, this is not the ideal time. It's probably not the optimal time to escalate much further than this unless it's absolutely necessary. And we're

talking here about certain strategic threats like the Hamas military infrastructure being destroyed or real ethnic cleansing, like with transfer. We haven't seen that yet, by the way, because the Israelis are grossly exaggerating the number of people in Northern Gaza fleeing to Southern Gaza. They want it to look like there's full ethnic cleansing already underway in order to flatten Northern Gaza. So there are many moving parts here. We still have to see where that's heading. If Hamas will be able to withstand the invasion on their own with Islamic Jihad, of course, and other factions, this has yet to be seen where, how that's going to play out.

But again, people are forgetting the Resistance Axis – yes, it's a new pole, if you like, in this new newly emerging multipolar world order – but it's still an asymmetric war, even with Iran, even with the PMU and Syria and Hizbullah and Hamas and the Yemenis, it's still the much weaker side from a material perspective, in terms of hard power. It's still the weaker side. It's still an asymmetric war. And so in asymmetric wars, unfortunately many more lives are sacrificed from the weaker side than from the stronger side. So it would ultimately be the weaker side that has to pay the price for this. And I think that's why Hizbullah is holding out until it's absolutely necessary. And there's a real threat that Gaza will fall, that Hamas will fall and other things like that.

LA: And I think an important thing to remember as well [is] I think some people, for understandable reasons, are perhaps, consciously or not, starting to conceive of Hizbullah as some kind of saviour, a saviour of Hamas, a saviour of Gaza in some way, whereas the reality is Hamas is a partner. They are strategic partners in constant and immediate communication. And so, I think, as you've just elaborated on, one of the dangers of that framing of 'why aren't they doing more?' is the reality that Hamas would be communicating to them if they really felt things were desperate.

AS: Yeah, we would be seeing that. And also Nasrallah himself last time and today actually talked about this, he said, this is not a battle we can just win in one decisive blow. It's about winning points, accumulating power. That's its strategy. And Hizbullah, and Iran and other actors, haven't always responded in kind to, like the assassination of [Qaseim] Soelimani, the assassination of [Imad] Mughniyeh. There have been many huge events that have happened that because they are the weaker side, have not been able in that moment to respond in kind. And this is why their response is always one of: we need more time to pass while we work on accumulating more power, work on developing our capabilities before we can respond in the appropriate way. Because there is no way you can respond to blows like that given the power differentials here. So I think it is something that will take time. Nasrallah himself, and that's why many people were upset today, he basically said, this is going to take time. He also alluded to an important point, I think, which is that Hizbullah is also binding it's time to see what happens inside Israel. And he [Nasrallah] said, let's watch the internal front there and let the pressure pile up on Netanyahu and his government. The hostages' families you've got all these rifts within Israel and these will all contribute in weakening the Israeli position a lot.

LA: Major economic problems as well.

AS: That's right. Economic. Demographic. For example, what's going to happen to all these settlements in the future as well. That's another thing – like where will all these [displaced] settlers go? Can they build more settlements in the future? Many things that we have to look at. So there's also this idea not just of exploding, the explosion kind of strategy from without, but for Israel to implode from within. And that's been a long, longstanding strategy of Hizbullah's as well. It's to combine both explosion and implosion.

LA: In his speech today as he's often forced to do, Nasrallah discussed military matters to some extent, and given Hizbullah is a military resistance organisation, amongst other things, and I know that you've had the opportunity to interview a number of senior military commanders of the party as part of your research, could you elaborate on something which you've already alluded to, but not fully expounded on, the enhanced, military capability of Hizbullah, notably in comparison to 2006 when it achieved its famous victory against Israel. How have things changed and developed in the almost 20 years since then?

AS: I don't get a lot of info from these interviews about weapons. They tend to be very tight-lipped about that. But in terms of tactics and strategy, so for example, in terms of strategy, we're seeing this today, which is what Hamas did on October 7, is the idea that it's an offensive defence strategy. And that's what we call forward defence. And this is an idea that Iran has adopted and Hizbullah has adopted, and clearly the Palestinian resistance factions as well, that they won't just sit on the defensive and wait for Israel to attack it. This is what I was referring to earlier as anticipatory self-defence, is that they will take the offensive and in fact, Hizbullah has been talking about this since the 2006 war, that the best defensive strategy is an offensive one. And I think that's the sort of prism through which we have to see all this now. So it's a shift from defence to offence, not just for Hizbullah, but for the entire resistance axis.

And now in terms of weapons, capabilities and tactics, this is all stuff that I find in different reports including Israeli and US reports and so on. So, for example, we know that according to all these reports and estimates that Hizbullah now has over 150,000 missiles. Whereas back in 2006, it had a total of 15,000 rockets. And its firepower for example, back in 2006, it was able to fire 4,000 rockets over 34 days. Whereas now the estimate is a minimum of 5,000 missiles daily. And they can also use this much larger arsenal in order to use saturation tactics to overwhelm Israeli air defences. You've got the Iron Dome and the David Sling and the Arrow system. So, there's a way that they could actually evade interception or many of these missiles, for example.

You also have, in terms of tactics here, I'm not talking about weapons here, but just tactics. Nasrallah himself has threatened repeatedly that Central Israel will be the target of any future war. In fact, if you recall, the Dahiyeh Doctrine that Israel had threatened to apply to all of Lebanon.

LA: For anyone who doesn't know what that is, could you just explain briefly?

AS: Yeah, so Dahiyeh is an area of Beirut. It's this sort of Shia-dominated area where the overwhelming majority of Hizbullah's support base, in addition to South Lebanon, resides, and Israel just basically destroyed it all. And then it was rebuilt, it threatened after 2006 to do the same to all of Lebanon, to where other sects live, Christians and Sunnis and Druze, and they called this the Dahiyeh Doctrine. In fact, they're implementing it today in Gaza. This is the Dahiyeh Doctrine being implemented.

So Nasrallah back then, back in after 2006 said it won't just be Dahiyeh for Haifa, it will be Dahiyeh doctrine vis-a-vis the Tel Aviv doctrine, which means Central Israel and Tel Aviv. And that's the new equation and that Hizbullah would respond by targeting civilian airports, military airports, air force bases. It could take out a lot of its [Israel's] air force, even if Hizbullah doesn't have sophisticated, for example, air defence systems and I know that it does have air defence systems, we just don't know how sophisticated they are, it can put, a lot of its air force out of service. It could hit power plants, Nasrallah threatened the Dimona nuclear reactor,

the Haifa power plant, the ammonia plant, sorry. It can hit water, desalination plants, central communication centres, oil refineries, pretty much everything. And back in 2006 it didn't target Tel Aviv, it hit Haifa and even then, like Haifa and the Northern settlements, it paralyzed Israel. So, the kind of damage it could inflict, and I'm not just talking about material damage, but for the economy, that would be beyond devastating, I would imagine, for Israel. As well as the fact that yes, Hizbullah does have much more sophisticated weapons now in terms of anti-tank guided missiles, anti-ship missiles. I read recently that Hizbullah has the Russian Yakhont anti-ship missile, which is supposed to be one of the most sophisticated of the lot. It's got all types of drones, short, medium, long range. Many of them are guided, some of them surveillance, some of them attack. Nasrallah alluded to this today as well in his speech.

Again, let's not forget the bunkers. Back in 2006, the bunkers were a crucial element in the war, and I can only imagine how many more kilometres of this network of tunnels Hizbullah has expanded. And we know even back in 2006, these were air conditioned, they had communications, everything. We've seen the Hamas tunnels, some footage of that. So again, I could only imagine what that would look like today as well. And in fact, Israel tried, I think it was 2019, through this operation called Northern Shield, they claimed that they destroyed a few of Hizbullah's tunnels, but then Nasrallah came out and said these were from before 2006 even and they're meaningless.

LA: And actually, and one thing I was just going to say that came to mind when you were talking about the kind of the enhanced capability is that as much as some people might be talking about Hizbullah as if they haven't intervened yet, they have actually already begun to use weapons which they've never actually used before, such as *Burkan* [rockets] and so things that had not previously been used and hadn't happened have now already begun to take place. And the other thing I was just going to ask in terms of manpower – that's been hugely increased since 2006, when actually a relatively small number of Hizbullah fighters were involved.

AS: Yes. Apparently, in my interviews, like from what I learned, there were only maybe 1,000 in direct combat back in 2006, there were a few thousand in total, maybe 4,000 or 5,000, and only 1,000 were in direct combat. So, in total it was around 5,000. And today we're talking about over 100,000 fighters including both full-time and reservists.

And also what we have to look at is a lot of these fighters are battle hardened now after Syria. So they have even more experience, not just fighting on Lebanese territory, but in Syria and Syrian territory too, which means not just urban warfare, but desert and mountain warfare experience. They fought in the snow under adverse weather conditions. They fought a counter-insurgency. So back in 2006, Hizbullah was a hybrid force [and] it fought a conventional army. But after they intervened in Syria, they were fighting a counter-insurgency against Isis and Al-Qaeda, and these are also hybrid forces, so it was a hybrid force fighting another hybrid force, using counterinsurgency methods. So Hizbullah is actually extremely versatile, militarily speaking. They also didn't have the elite Radwan Force back in 2006, which are Hizbullah's special commando units named after al-Hajj Radwan, Imad Mughniyeh, and in fact this whole new school of fighting that Mughniyeh introduced in 2006 has only but developed over the years and has turned what was a formidable hybrid force in 2006, this new school of fighting, as they call it, into something even bigger now. The many lessons learned from the war in Syria, what they're observing now in Gaza as well, the different tactics. So in the past we used to talk about Hizbullah infiltrating from Galilee, and they have a special unit, an offensive unit that is trained to do just that. But, Nasrallah himself said that wouldn't be all that Hizbullah would do. They're not just going to rely on infiltration, and in fact, you've got a hundred kilometres of border. And so there would have to be a lot of this done actually through valleys and hills, he said. And so he says, I've written the quote here: 'they do not know how we will enter, from above the ground, below the ground, coming down on them from the sky, from several metre heights.' So again, there are many different ways that Hizbullah will participate in this using different methods. But there will definitely be an offensive of Hizbullah entering occupied Palestine. It's not just going to be [a case] of long range or short range or medium range missiles hitting Israel. I don't think it's simply going to be that, like what we saw in 2006.

LA: Something that you mentioned earlier on is that obviously there is the potential that such a military confrontation, especially right now, given what we've seen the US send to the region over the last month, that confrontation could entail direct confrontation with US forces. And something that Nasrallah has stressed for a number of years, as far as I could tell, going back over a decade at least, is that, and especially in his speech on November 3rd, is that it is the US that bears the ultimate responsibility for Israel's actions and its repeated massacres and outrages. I would say that his analysis of the dynamic between Israel and the US is essentially a materialist, anti-imperialist position. And more than once, actually, he's spoken in detail about the nature of US imperialist hegemony generally. As just a quick example of something that he said. I think this was in 2015, he said:

> in the project of American hegemony, it is not permitted for a strong state to exist. A strong state in the sense of an independent state, a state that makes its de-

cisions on its own. A country that takes into account the interest of its people. A country that benefits from and employs its resources and its economy. A state that develops scientifically, technically, culturally, and administratively at every level. In the project of American hegemony, such a state is forbidden.

So could you maybe elaborate on this position and how it developed within the party and why?

AS: It's interesting because I've actually written this in my first book on Hizbullah, which was published 2002, where I did the sort of rank ordering of Hizbullah's oppressor category. And they used to place Israel at the top. And the idea was the analogy of the serpent, that Israel was the serpent's head and the US was its back, and that the tail was the sort of unjust Lebanese state at the time before the Ta'if agreement [1989]. So, this has shifted a lot over the years actually, and Hizbullah, no longer adopts this type of hierarchy of evil, if you like. Iran, by the way, for a long time, has referred to Israel as the small Satan and the US as the big Satan.

LA: I thought Britain was the small Satan, maybe Britain's the tiny Satan now.

AS: Nasrallah actually alluded to Britain just being like a follower of the US in a very dismissive tone.

I think this change really started in 2006, especially after it became very clear to Hizbullah that the US was behind the war. And then of course you had the Seymour Hirsch article about the US' role and how it engineered the whole invasion at the time. And so Hizbullah on its own as well, came to the understanding that Israel was doing the US' bidding really in 2006. So the discourse started to shift.

LA: Just one thing on that, in case people aren't aware – it was revealed that it was very much Bush and the US administration that were refusing a ceasefire.

AS: Yeah. Much like they are now, right?

LA: Exactly. And again, then as now the UK fully backed that position.

AS: The language then was different. I recall. It's much more brazen today. The rejection of the ceasefire, they simply say now, like all gloves are off, no ceasefire, it will embolden Hamas. Back in 2006, they used to use more indirect references, like we need to see the conditions that can sustain a ceasefire. So, it was the same result, obviously, but just more shy. Although it was a Republican government and it was Bush for God's sake, still it was less harsh than Biden's administration. Anyway, so back in 2006, that discourse started to shift and then Hizbullah issued a new manifesto in 2009. So it updated its open letter of 1985, and in that manifesto, it specifically refers to American-led, Israeli-executed wars on the resistance in Lebanon and Palestine. So the idea of Israeli invasions were no longer divorced from the US and Israel was seen as simply executing American-engineered invasions and military campaigns against the Palestinians and Lebanese, so that became a more refined understanding of the way this relationship works. And then there's a 2012 interview, it's actually been going round on Twitter, I was reminded of this interview, which is very important, Nasrallah said that the idea of a Zionist lobby controlling US politics was a myth and that in fact it's a trinity of the arms industry, oil and Christian Zionists and that Israel is but a tool of the US in all this. So again, that idea developed further over the years. And now of course, Nasrallah repeatedly talked about how Israel is in fact a proxy of the US – an instrument, a tool. You know how it's a settler colony [and] is the West's last remaining outpost in the world today, in fact, and that's why it's clinging onto it for their life.

So, there's this very different view of Israel that's emerged over the years that it is in fact something that was developed because of facts on the ground. The battlefield is how this developed. They've come to realise, I think, and there's a real belief now, I think, among the different resistance actors in this axis that Israel is in fact, very weak. And I don't think that the US' intervention today did it any favours in terms of making it look – forget about invincible, that myth was shattered in 2006 by Hizbullah and then repeatedly after, by Hamas and Islamic Jihad and Palestine – but there's like a very different view today of Israel, as I think you wrote about this, Louis, about how it's just like a kind of unsustainable settler colony, like Rhodesia, [and] that one day this regime could fall. And there is this sort of awareness, I would say, among many now that this could happen. It could happen. It's feasible.

LA: Yeah. And I think that takes us back to where we started actually, in terms of how in addition to the literal battle there is also this battle of awareness, consciousness, ideas, and I think a key component of that is, as you said, there was a point during the Israeli occupation of Lebanon that fighting it and defeating it and kicking it out felt like an absurd, impossible thing, and I think you can extrapolate from that, that even now, notwithstanding the current crisis that Israel is in and the weakness – in spite of the immeasurable suffering it is currently inflicting – despite the weakness it has shown, I think many people would still struggle to envisage a scenario where Israel ceases to exist as Israel, as an ethnocratic, Jewish supremacist, settler colony. And I think probably part of the struggle that he's referring to when he talks about that is getting people to conceptualise that as a possibility, if not an eventuality. Even if, as he said today, it's not going to be quick. And actually, that was something I wanted to ask you – when Nasrallah says that, what do you, and I don't want you to predict things that, no one can really predict in a way, but when he says it's going to be long, what do you think is meant by that? Are we talking one year, two years, five years? Do you think there's a vision for what that looks like?

AS: I think the idea of the Great War – this is what Hizbullah's referred to it as for a while now, and the one that they've been envisaging since 2006 – will be the last war and will be a great war because it will necessarily be regional, maybe even international now that the US and other powers have stepped in. And because it is going to be an extremely destructive war, it will take time to get to that point the Resistance Axis builds the capabilities it needs to be able to wage that war. And I think it's important also to think that, as we said, this is no longer a case of purely defensive strategy, but one that's forward defence or offensive defence. And I don't see why that would change. I think it would be one that might be initiated by any one of these actors. It will probably be initiated by them, but at a time that is more appropriate, whether that's Hizbullah or by Hamas or Islamic Jihad, or whomever. And because it's going to take a bit of time I think that's why he's keeping it ambiguous, obviously, as well, aside from the element of surprise. But I do think all actors, or in this axis, all the allies have been preparing for this for years, as they prepared for [something like] Hamas' October 7th attack. They have been preparing for this for years, but I don't think this is something that will happen decades from now. No, I think we're talking about the shorter term. And it's, this is just obviously my own prediction, I do believe it's something that will happen in my lifetime if I live long enough. I don't think it's something that's going to necessarily be very long term.

LA: Exactly, I didn't want to put you on the spot for a number because there are so many factors, foremost amongst them the broader global position. And if a regional war did begin, how would Russia and China react to that? What would the Saudi position be? There are so many interconnected factors that I think predicting things with certainty would be a fool's errand.

AS: Yeah. I'm not even thinking about powers like Russia and China and I don't think that the Resistance Axis sits there awaiting their assistance to be honest. But I do think this is obviously something that's going to be done independent of these other powers where they're going to stand if and when the time comes. And I think it's not if, it's when, but one which as Nasrallah has repeatedly said, it's going to take time, there needs to be more readiness. They are ready now. I do think they're ready. I don't think Hamas would have done this if they didn't anticipate a very strong Israeli response. And this is something that happened to Hizbullah in 2006. Yes, they didn't expect Israel to respond in the very, very aggressive way it did to the abduction of two of its soldiers. But they did plan for that scenario, and I think it's the same today. I'm pretty confident actually, if not more, that because of 2006 and other invasions after that, that Hamas and others in this alliance knew that, I'm not saying that they knew exactly when this was going to happen, Iran and Hizbullah, I'm just saying that they had obviously been training and helping Hamas to plan for this, and Islamic Jihad. But they knew that Israel would respond because it always responds like this, it responds like this, whether the targets are military or civilian or whomever. It responds with the Dahiyeh doctrine, right? That's how it's been responding for many years now. So they must have predicted this would happen.

No one knows at this point for how long this is going to drag on. No one knows what the US is actually, where it's heading with this. And the US has been lying a lot. Like the Biden administration has been giving a lot of mixed signals in terms of, for example, ethnic cleansing. One day they say, we don't want this, and then we find out that in fact it was a US idea to transfer the Gaza population to Sinai. So we don't know really what the US' intentions are or how seriously it's taking this threat of opening another front from Israel's Northern Front and other actors, we don't know. But what I do think is they must have anticipated a scenario where this is going to drag on for a long time, and that Hamas might reach a point where it starts to, I don't know, run out of weapons or resources or whatever. Then what would happen? There must be a contingency plan to make this a regional war.

LA: We've covered a lot in quite a short space of time there, Amal, so I think this is a good point to wrap things up. I know you are currently working on finishing your next book about Hizbullah. Do you want to just say a quick word about that and when it's out?

AS: I have to finish it this year, my publisher won't let me extend it anymore. Inshallah late summer I will have finished it and then it will go into production and I've got a lot to update and add now because of what's going on. It's actually quite overwhelming how many things I've got to add now to each chapter. Yeah, it's just a lot. But I think it's going to be especially pertinent now, the title is Resistance Axis.

LA: Hizbullah and the Resistance Axis is one of those topics where there are a lot of very bad 'experts' and a lot of really bad 'expertise,' so it's been a pleasure to talk with someone who actually is an expert. Thank you very much for your time, Amal.

AS: Thanks for having me, Louis.

The Palestinians' Inalienable Right to Resist

Louis Allday

Editor's note: this article was originally published in June 2021.

> We remembered all the miseries, all the injustices, our people and the conditions they lived, the coldness with which world opinion looks at our cause, and so we felt that we will not permit them to crush us. We will defend ourselves and our revolution by every way and every means.
> – George Habash

> A freedom fighter learns the hard way that it is the oppressor who defines the nature of the struggle, and the oppressed is often left no recourse but to use methods that mirror those of the oppressor.
> – Nelson Mandela

In December 1982, following Israel's devastating invasion of Lebanon six months earlier, the United Nations General Assembly passed resolution A/RES/37/43 concerning the '[i]mportance of the universal realisation of the right of peoples to self-determination'. It endorsed, without qualification, 'the inalienable right' of the Palestinian people to 'self-determination, national independence, territorial integrity, national unity and sovereignty without outside interference', and reaffirmed the legitimacy of their struggle for those rights 'by all available means, including armed struggle'. It also strongly condemned Israel's 'expansionist activities in the Middle East' and 'continual bombing of Palestinian civilians', both said to 'constitute a serious obstacle to the realisation of the self-determination and independence of the Palestinian people'. In the four decades since then, Israel's violence against the Palestinian people and its colonisation of their land has not ceased. Up to the present moment, all over historical Palestine, from the Gaza Strip to Sheikh Jarrah, Palestinians are still under that same occupation, subject to suffocating control over virtually every aspect of their lives – and the sadistic, unaccountable violence of the Zionist state.

In addition to its endorsement by the UN, the Palestinians' right to resist their occupation is also guaranteed by international law. The Fourth Geneva Convention requires an occupying power to protect the 'status quo, human rights and prospects for self-determination' of occupied populations, and as Richard Falk – an expert in international law who later went on to be appointed the UN's Special Rapporteur on Human Rights in the Occupied Palestinian Territories – has explained, Israel's 'pronounced, blatant and undisguised' refusal to ever accept this framework of legal obligations constitutes a fundamental denial of the Palestinians' right to self-determination and engenders their legally-protected right of resistance.[1] Israel's occupation of Palestinian territory and its flagrant disregard for international law through the construction of illegal settlements and other daily violations has continued unabated since Falk's assessment was made during the al-Aqsa Intifada. In fact, the occupation has only become further entrenched since then with the collaboration of the comprador Palestinian Authority.

Furthermore, regardless of what is mandated by international law, the Palestinians possess a fundamental moral right to resist their ongoing colonisation and oppression through armed resistance, and that right must be recognised and supported. The multi-generational suffering of the Palestinians, perhaps none more so than those who live in the besieged and bombarded Gaza strip, is unremittingly cruel and has one central cause: Israel and the perpetual belligerence, expansionism and racism that is inherent to its state ideology, Zionism. Moreover, contrary to the Western media's narrative that, without fail, portrays Israel as acting in 'retaliation', it is the actions of the Palestinians which are fundamentally reactive in nature, because the violence that Israel inflicts upon them is both perpetual and structural, and therefore automatically precedes any resistance to it. 'With the establishment of a relationship of oppression, violence has already begun', said Paolo Freire; '[n]ever in history has violence been initiated by the oppressed'. In Palestine, as Ali Abunimah recently wrote, 'the root cause of all political violence is Zionist colonisation'.[2]

Given that the Palestinians' legal and moral right to pursue armed resistance is clear, endorsement of this position should be uncontroversial and commonplace among supporters of their cause. Yet in the West, such a position is rarely expressed – even by those who loudly proclaim their solidarity with Palestine. On the contrary, acts of Palestinian armed resistance, such as the firing of missiles from Gaza, are condemned by these ostensible supporters as part of the problem, dismissed condescendingly as 'futile' and 'counter-productive', or even labelled 'war crimes' and 'unthinkable atrocities', said to be comparable to Israel's routine collective punishment, torture, incarceration, bombardment and murder of Palestinians. This form of solidarity, as Bikrum Gill has argued, is essentially 'premised upon re-inscribing Palestinians as inherently non-sovereign beings who can only be recognised as disempowered dependent objects to be acted upon, either by Israeli colonial violence, or white imperial protectors'.[3]

To sit in the comfort and safety of the West and condemn acts of armed resistance that the Palestinians choose to carry out – always at great risk to their lives – is a deeply chauvinistic position. It must be stated plainly: it is not the place of those who choose to stand in solidarity with the Palestinians from afar to then try and dictate how they should wage the anti-colonial struggle that, as Frantz Fanon believed, is necessary to maintain their humanity and dignity, and ultimately to achieve their liberation. Those who are not under brutal military occupation or refugees from ethnic cleansing have no right to judge the manner in which those who are choose to confront their colonisers. Indeed, expressing solidarity with the Palestinian cause is ultimately meaningless if that support dissipates the moment that the Palestinians resist their oppression with anything more than rocks and can no longer be portrayed as courageous, photogenic, but ultimately powerless, victims. 'Does the world expect us to offer ourselves up as polite, willing and well-mannered sacrifices, who are murdered without raising a single objection?' Yahya al-Sinwar, Hamas' leader in Gaza, recently asked rhetorically. 'This is not possible. No, we have decided to defend our people with whatever strength we have been given'.[4]

This phenomenon speaks to what Jones Manoel calls the Western left's 'fetish for defeat' that predisposes it towards situations 'of oppression, suffering and martyrdom', as opposed to successful acts of resistance and revolution. Manoel continues:

> People become ecstatic looking at those images – which I don't think are very fantastic – of a [Palestinian] child or teenager using a sling to launch a rock at a tank. Look, this is a clear example of heroism but it is also a symbol of barbarism. This is a people who do not have the capacity to defend themselves facing an imperialist colonial power that is armed to the teeth. They do not have an equal capacity of resistance, but this is romanticised.[5]

As a result, large swathes of the Western left express solidarity with the Palestinian cause in a generalised, abstract way, overstating the importance of their own role, and simultaneously rejecting the very groups who are currently fighting – and dying – for it. All too often, those who have refused to surrender and steadfastly resisted at great cost, are condemned by people who, in the same breath, declare solidarity with the cause. Similarly, it is common for these same people to either ignore or demonise those external forces that materially aid the Palestinian resistance more than any others – most notably Iran. If this assistance is acknowledged, which is rare, the Palestinian groups that accept it are typically infantilised as mere 'dupes' or 'pawns', for allowing themselves to be used cynically by the self-serving acts of others – a sentiment that directly contradicts Palestinian leaders' own statements.

A specific criticism of Hamas that is frequently deployed in this context is the 'in-discriminate' nature of its missile launches from Gaza, actions which both Human Rights Watch and Amnesty International regularly label 'war crimes'. As observed by Perugini and Gordon, the false equivalence that this designation relies upon 'essentially says that using homemade missiles – there isn't much else available to people living under permanent siege – is a war crime. In other words, Palestinian armed groups are criminalised for their technological inferiority'.[6] After the latest round of fighting in May 2021, al-Sinwar stated clearly that, unlike Israel, 'which possesses a complete arsenal of weaponry, state-of-the-art equipment and aircraft' and 'bombs our children and women, on purpose', if Hamas possessed 'the capabilities to launch precision missiles that targeted military targets, we wouldn't have used the rockets that we did. We are forced to defend our people with what we have, and this is what we have'.[7]

This failure to support legitimate armed struggle is a part of a wider problem with the framing used by many supporters of the Palestinian cause in the West, that obscures its fundamental nature and how it must be resolved. Palestine is not simply a human rights issue, or even just a question of apartheid, but rather an anti-colonial fight for national liberation being waged by an indigenous resistance against the forces of an imperialist-backed settler colony. Decolonisation is a word now frequently used in the West in an abstract sense or in relation to curricula, institutions and public art, but rarely anymore in connection to what actually matters most: land. And that is the very crux of the issue: the land of Palestine must be decolonised, its Zionist colonisers deposed, their racist structures and barriers – both physical and political – dismantled, and all Palestinian refugees given the right of return.

It should be noted that emphasising the importance of supporting the Palestinians' right to carry out armed struggle in pursuit of their freedom does not mean that their supporters in the West should recklessly call for violence or fetishise and celebrate it unnecessarily. Nor does it mean that non-violent efforts such as the Boycott, Divestment and Sanctions Movement (BDS) are inconsequential or unimportant. Rather, BDS should be considered part and parcel of a broad spectrum of resistance activities, of which armed struggle is an integral component. Samah Idriss, founding member of the Campaign to Boycott Supporters of Israel in Lebanon has stated: '[b]oth forms of resistance, civil and armed, are complementary and should not be viewed as mutually exclusive.'[8] Or, as Khaled Barakat has stressed: 'Israel and its allies have never accepted any form of Palestinian resistance, and boycott campaigns and popular organising are not alternatives to armed resistance but interdependent tactics of struggle'.[9]

Nelson Mandela's analysis is relevant in this context, when he wrote that, '[n]on-violent passive resistance is effective as long as your opposition adheres to the same rules as you do', but if peaceful protest is met with violence, its efficacy is at an end'.[10] For Mandela, 'non-violence was not a moral principle but a strategy', since 'there is no moral goodness in using an ineffective weapon'. Clarifying the rationale behind the African National Congress' decision to adopt armed resistance, Mandela explained that it had no alternative course left available: '[o]ver and over again, we had used all the non-violent weapons in our arsenal – speeches, deputations, threats, marches, strikes, stay-aways, voluntary imprisonment – all to no avail, for whatever we did was met by an iron hand'. This standpoint is reflected in the words of al-Sinwar, who when referring to the Great March of Return protests in 2018-19, during which Israeli snipers shot dead hundreds of Gazan protestors and seriously wounded thousands more said: 'we've tried peaceful

resistance and popular resistance', but rather than acting to stop Israel's massacres, 'the world stood by and watched as the occupation war machine killed our young people'.[11]

Mandela's reference to efficacy is crucial. Despite what many Western supporters seem intent on implying, although it comes at a huge cost, the Palestinian armed resistance in Gaza is not 'futile' and has grown enormously in effectiveness and deterrent capacity. This was already evident after Israel's failure to win the 2014 war on Gaza and has been underlined by the recent success of the resistance in May 2021, during which it launched an unprecedented number of missiles that can now reach deep inside historical Palestine. In spite of its devastating aerial bombardment of Gaza, Israel was unable to stop the launch of these missiles and, after the losses it experienced in 2014, is now too fearful of launching another ground invasion of the strip – notably as the resistance is now equipped with greater numbers of Kornet missiles previously used to such deadly effect against Israeli tanks in Southern Lebanon. The ceasefire that was declared on May 21st [2021] was widely seen in Israel as a defeat, and was celebrated by Palestinians across historical Palestine as a victory. The military balance has changed, and although Israel is still vastly more powerful by every conventional measure, the resistance is in a stronger position now than it has been for years. It has built upon the successes of Hezbollah against Israel in 2000 and 2006 and with the support, training and further aid of the Lebanese group and others in the Resistance Axis, it has taken its capabilities to a higher level. This change is reflected in the fact that since 2014, Israeli arms sales have stagnated and its aggressions against Gaza no longer lead to an immediate rise in the stock price of its arms companies that use Gaza as a training ground and stage for its latest technologies. Shir Hever has noted that after Israel's failures in Gaza beginning in 2014, customers of its arms companies began to ask 'What is the point of all this technology? If you cannot pacify the Palestinians with these missiles, why should we buy them?'.[12]

In addition to its practical impact, armed struggle has significant propaganda value. The reality is that Palestine would not have dominated global news headlines in May 2021 in the way that it did were it not for the armed resistance in Gaza that – contrary to the Western media's singular focus on Hamas – is composed of a united front of various factions including Palestinian Islamic Jihad (PIJ) and the Marxist-Leninist Popular Front for the Liberation of Palestine (PFLP). The PFLP is a case in point in this regard, for it was their actions throughout the late 1960s and early 1970s, most notably a series of plane hijackings (in which passengers were released unharmed), that implanted the Palestinian cause in the consciousness of millions of people for the first time and marked a key turning point in raising awareness of the Palestinians' plight globally. Indeed, the Palestinian writer and PFLP spokesman, Ghassan Kanafani, believed that armed struggle was the 'best form of propaganda' and that in spite of the 'gigantic propaganda system of the United States', it is through people who fight to liberate themselves in armed struggle 'that things are ultimately decided'.[13]

In 1970, after the Western-backed regime in Jordan had shelled Palestinian refugee camps in the country, the PFLP – under the leadership of Kanafani's comrade (and recruiter) George Habash – took hostage a group of nationals from the US, West Germany and Britain (Israel's primary supporters) at two hotels in Amman. In return for their safe release, the PFLP demanded that 'all shelling of the camps be ended and all demands of the Palestinian resistance movement met'. Shortly before the hostages were eventually released, Habash addressed them apologetically and said:

I feel that it's my duty to explain to you why we did what we did. Of course, from a liberal point of view of thinking, I feel sorry for what happened, and I am sorry that we caused you some trouble during the last 2 or 3 days. But leaving this aside, I hope that you will understand, or at least try to understand, why we did what we did.

Maybe it will be difficult for you to understand our point of view. People living different circumstances think on different lines. They can't think in the same manner, and we, the Palestinian people, and the conditions we have been living for a good number of years, all these conditions have modelled our way of thinking. We can't help it. You can understand our way of thinking, when you know a very basic fact. We, the Palestinians... for the last 22 years, have been living in camps and tents. We were driven out of our country, our houses, our homes and our lands, driven out like sheep and left here in refugee camps in very inhumane conditions.

For 22 years our people have been waiting in order to restore their rights, but nothing happened... After 22 years of injustice, inhumanity, living in camps with nobody caring for us, we feel that we have the very full right to protect our revolution. We have all the right to protect our revolution...

We don't wake up in the morning to have a cup of milk with Nescafe and then spend half an hour before the mirror thinking of flying to Switzerland or having one month in this country or one month in that country... We live daily in camps... We can't be calm as you can. We can't think as you think. We have lived in this condition, not for one day, not for 2 days, not for 3 days. Not for one week, not for 2 weeks, not for 3 weeks. Not for one year, not for 2 years, but for 22 years. If any one of you comes to these camps and stays for one or two weeks, he will be affected.

You have to excuse my English. From the personal side, let me say, I apologise to you. I am sorry about your troubles for 3 or 4 days. But from a revolutionary point of view, we feel, we will continue to feel that we have the very, very full right to do what we did.

Habash's words should be listened to carefully. The urgency that underlines his message is even more palpable half a century later, for the Palestinians – consistently refusing passive victimhood – have now lived in the wretched conditions Habash depicts for 73 long years, not 22.

Revolution, Mao Zedong once remarked, 'is not a dinner party, or writing an essay, or painting a picture, or doing embroidery; it cannot be so refined, so leisurely and gentle'. The same is true of decolonisation, in which although past struggles have been multi-faceted, armed resistance of some kind was almost invariably an integral component of the struggle. Palestine is no exception. Beyond endorsement of BDS and other civil society campaigns, the Palestinians' unassailable right to pursue armed struggle must be supported by those who choose to stand in solidarity with them and their righteous cause.

References

1   Richard Falk, 'International Law and the al-Aqsa Intifada', *MERIP*, Winter 2000.

2   Ali Abunimah, 'It's time to change liberal discourse about Hamas', *The Electronic Intifada*, 2021.

3   Bikrum Gill (@bikrumsinghgill), Twitter/X, 20 May 2021.

4   Yahya al-Sinwar, Interview with *Vice News*, May 2021.

5   Jones Manoel, 'Western Marxism Loves Purity and Martyrdom, But Not Real Revolution', *Black Agenda Report*, 2020.

6   Nicola Perugini and Neve Gordon, 'How Amnesty International Criminalises Palestinians for Their Inferior Weapons', *Counterpunch*, 2015.

7   Yahya al-Sinwar, Interview with *Vice News*, 2021.

8   As quoted in Khaled Barakat, 'Uphold Palestinian struggle in all its forms', *Electronic Intifada*, 2020.

9   Khaled Barakat, 'Uphold Palestinian struggle in all its forms', *Electronic Intifada*, 2020.

10   This and the following Mandela quotes are all from an e-book of his 1994 autobiography, *Long Walk to Freedom*.

11   Yahya al-Sinwar, Interview with *Vice News*, 2021.

12   "Who Rules Israel – Shir Hever Part 2", *theAnalysis-News* (YouTube), 3 June 2021.

13   As quoted in the 1971 film *The Red Army/PFLP: Declaration of World War* directed by Masao Adachi & Kôji Wakamatsu.

'Our Code of Morals is Our Revolution': On Morality and the Palestinian Revolution

George Habash

In June 1970, after the Western-backed regime in Jordan had shelled Palestinian refugee camps in the country, the Popular Front for the Liberation of Palestine (PFLP), under the leadership of its Secretary General, George Habash, took a group of nationals from the USA, West Germany and Britain – Israel's primary sponsors – hostage at two hotels in the capital, Amman.

In return for their safe release, the PFLP demanded that 'all shelling of the camps be ended and all demands of the Palestinian resistance movement met'. Shortly before the hostages were all safely released a few days later on June 12th 1970, Habash addressed them in person at the Jordan Intercontinental Hotel in Amman and thoughtfully explained the group's actions from a Palestinian revolutionary perspective.

Habash's words – published in full below – should be listened to very carefully, especially by those who sympathise with the Palestinian cause but waver in their solidarity when the Palestinians dare to fight back. The unprecedented armed resistance launched by Hamas and the united factions in Gaza – of which the PFLP is one – in October 2023 must be understood in the context that Habash so eloquently describes.

The urgency that underlines his message is even more palpable half a century later, for the Palestinians – consistently refusing passive victimhood – have now lived in the wretched conditions Habash depicts for 75 long years, not 22.

Ladies and gentlemen;

I feel that it is my duty to explain to you why we did what we did. Of course, from a liberal point of view of thinking, I feel sorry for what happened, and I am sorry that we caused you some trouble during the last 2 or 3 days. But leaving this aside, I hope that you will understand, or at least try to understand, why we did what we did. Maybe it will be difficult for you to understand our point of view. People living different circumstances think on different lines. They cannot think in the same manner and we, the Palestinian people, and the conditions we have been living for a good number of years, all these conditions have modelled our way of thinking. We cannot help it. You can understand our way of thinking when you know a very basic fact. We, the Palestinians for 22 years, for the last 22 years, have been living in camps and tents. We were driven out of our country, our houses, our homes and our lands, driven out like sheep and left here in refugee camps in very inhumane conditions. For 22 years our people have been waiting in order to restore their rights but nothing happened. Three years ago circumstances became favourable so that our people could carry arms to defend their cause and start to fight to restore their rights, to go back to their country and liberate their country. After 22 years of injustice, inhumanity, living in camps with nobody caring for us, we feel that we have the very full right to protect our revolution. We have all the right to protect our revolution. Our code of morals is our revolution. What saves our revolution, what helps our revolution, what protects our revolution is right, is very right and very honourable and very noble and very beautiful, because our revolution means justice, means having back our homes, having back our country, which is a very just and noble aim. You have to take this point into consideration. If you want to be, in one way or another, co-operative with us, try to understand our point of view.

We don't wake up in the morning to have a cup of milk with Nescafe and then spend half an hour before the mirror thinking of flying to Switzerland or having one month in this country or one month in that country. We don't have the thousands or millions of dollars that you in America and Britain have. We live daily in camps. Our wives wait for the water, whether it will come at 10 o'clock in the morning, 12 o'clock or 3 o'clock in the afternoon. We cannot be calm, as you can. We cannot think as you think.

We have lived in this condition, not for one day, not for two days, not for three days. Not for one week, not for two weeks, not for three weeks. Not for one year, not for two years, but *for 22 years.*

If any one of you comes to these camps and stays for one or two weeks, he will be affected. He cannot think and handle things regardless of the conditions he will be living.

When our revolution started three years ago, so many attempts were planned to strike our revolution. Actually all commando organisations after June 1967, a very well-

known date to you, started and their eyes aimed at the conquered land. But when the revolution went on, so many forces – our enemies – put so many plans to beat this revolution. America is against us. We know this very well. We feel this very well. We felt it last year from the aid of the Phantoms. America is against our revolution. They work to crush our revolution. They work through the reactionary regime in Jordan and the reactionary regime in Lebanon. They tried on the fourth of November in 1968 to crush the revolution. Nevertheless, during events here, all of us were aiming for the conquered land. This was the first attempt on the 4th of November 1968. A second attempt, four months ago, on the tenth of February and during the last week, we lived the 3rd attempt. Actually, they are working daily against the revolution, every day. These dates are the peaks only, when their attempts reached a certain high level. Every time we lose men, we lose blood, we give sacrifices. On the 10th of February there was something like 50 casualties, at least. Regarding this third attempt from the reactionary regime to smash the revolution – and people who live here in Jordan know it very well and feel it very well – the reactionary regime started this. Anybody who lives in Jordan knows this very well. We cannot base our revolution on lies. I am talking facts here.

Last Saturday there was an incident here in Amman. On Sunday there was an incident in Zerqa, and then things flared. This time we felt, to be frank with you, that this attempt, at least from their own point of view, seems to be the final attempt. I mean to say, we felt that this time they are determined to smash the revolution no matter what level the sacrifices were.

Here, we felt that we have all the right in the world to protect our revolution. We remembered all the miseries, all the injustices, our people and the conditions they lived, the coldness with which world opinion looks at our case, and so we felt that we will not permit them to crush us. We will defend ourselves and our revolution by every way and every means, because – as I told you – our code of morals is our revolution. Anything that protects our revolution would be right. This is our line of thinking. So we put counterplans deciding that we should win.

One of the items in this plan was what happened here. We felt that we have the full right to make pressure here on the reactionary regime and in America and all forces, and this will be a winning card in our hand. I am talking very frankly and I have also to be frank and tell you something. We were really determined. We were not joking.

I am so glad that things and conditions went the way they should, because – to be frank – we were fully determined that, in case they will smash us in the camps, we will blow all this building and the Philadelphia [Hotel] all over. We were really determined to do this: Why? Because we know that our revolution will continue even if they crush us here in Amman and we want your governments to know that from now on the Front will mean every word it says.

We were fully determined to blow this hotel and the Philadelphia Hotel on one condition and in one circumstance. We were very keen not to lose our nerves. We were very keen not to lose our nerves. They were very determined, by their tanks, artillery and airplanes, to smash us. You are not better than our people. In the last incidents there were something like 500 casualties, the least number, believe me, the least number.

Yesterday I was in one hospital only, where the doctors told me that there are 280 wounded and 60 dead. Dead fighters.

Ladies and gentlemen;

I feel so much released now that we were not put in the corner and forced to do all that we were determined to do in case conditions went in that way.

I know the liberal way of thinking. I know it very well. I know how much it would be difficult to convince you. I know that some of you will be saying at present: 'What have I to do with these conditions? This is very unfair and very unjust and rude and selfish.' All right.

Conditions in which people live – these conditions, actually, determine their way of thinking and code of morals.

We tried our best – and I hope we succeeded in this – that during your presence in the hotel under the auspices of the Front, that you would be treated the best way we can.

This is the first time we manage a hotel. Our men, I am sure, know how to fight very well, but I don't know to what extent they were good at managing the hotel. But instructions were very clear. I hope they succeeded in this. I think we always helped you by keeping our nerves. The day before yesterday, Al-Wahdat Camp was shelled for more than half an hour. Anyone of you can go to Al-Wahdat Camp and see the places affected. It is very natural to start thinking [at] that time of executing the item. We held our nerves very well.

Ladies and gentlemen;

You have to excuse my English. From the personal side, let me say, I apologise to you. I am sorry about your troubles for three or four days. But from a revolutionary point of view, we feel, we will continue to feel that we have the very, very full right to do what we did.

Thank you very much.

George Habash (1926-2008) was a Palestinian physician, politician and revolutionary. Habash was one of the founders of the Movement of Arab Nationalists in 1951 and later the Popular Front for the Liberation of Palestine in 1967.

Direct Action and the Global Fight Against Israel's Arms Industry

Liam Doherty

On November 18th 2023, the UN-affiliated Al-Fakhoura school in the Jabalia refugee camp, northern Gaza, was bombed by the Israeli military. Thousands of hungry, thirsty and injured Gazans had been sheltering inside, having been displaced from their recently levelled homes. Fifty Palestinians were killed, and it was impossible to retrieve many bodies from the rubble. Bombing attacks like this have characterised the genocide underway against Palestinians in Gaza, which by the time of the Al-Fakhoura massacre had already claimed the lives of 12,000 Palestinians.

A month prior to the bombing, the Workers in Palestine coalition of over thirty trade unions issued an urgent call to stop arming Israel, to refuse the manufacture and transport of weapons for Israel, and to take action against complicit companies involved in implementing Israel's brutal and illegal siege.[1] This letter has set out clearly that there are important, material actions that can be taken by people of conscience to address this 'urgent, genocidal situation', a situation in which the arms trade plays a central role.

In response to Israel's ethnic cleansing and brutal massacres, protests have erupted across the globe with levels of participation and a diversity of locations rarely seen before. Israel's attacks on Gaza and the West Bank have drawn people in their millions to stand against the genocide, and as a result

there are more people ready to take action in support of Palestinian liberation. Still, the industries and institutions enabling these atrocities are able to continue operating, isolated from the democratic demands for their cessation. The question for the international solidarity effort, then, is how do we mobilise people towards practical resistance? Activism ought to focus on moving the conversation from one of humanitarian sympathy for Palestinians to one of accountability, critically examining our countries' roles in these atrocities and acting accordingly.

It is beyond doubt that we in the West are culpable for what is taking place in Gaza. Almost all of the tens of thousands of bombs dropped so far have been US-made Mk80 types, delivered using F-16 fighter-bombers. These are US-made with many British components – supported by drones, helmets, and communications technologies and more – that are manufactured across Britain, the US, and EU. Israel's bombing attacks rely extensively on Western-made weapons and weapons components.

Importantly, these arms sales and transfers are happening in real time. In addition to offering support for Israel's ethnic cleansing campaign in Gaza, our governments are continuing to arm this campaign with new Western-produced military equipment and weaponry. The US is sending security assistance on a near-daily basis to Israel. The Netherlands has made a new shipment of

F-35 fighter jet components, despite the certainty of their use against Gaza's besieged population.[2] Germany has announced record arms exports to Israel, with hundreds of new permits granted for weapons shipments this year – the majority of them since October 7th 2023. Britain, meanwhile, is facilitating the shipment of arms to Israel through its RAF bases, as well as continuing to approve weapons exports to the occupation.

Despite spending decades accumulating these weapons, Israel needs more. With 25,000 tonnes of bombs dropped in a month, the campaign has been hugely costly for the occupation. Israel had already seen the depletion of the US weapons stockpiles that it hosts, much of which was diverted to Ukraine throughout 2022. Stockpiles of precision munitions are low, and Israel is desperate to procure artillery shells, small diameter bombs, joint direct attack munitions and Hellfire missiles from its US and European allies. This gives activists in the West an opportunity: to disrupt the flow of these weapons, and to curtail Israel's ability to commit these atrocities.

If the question, then, is one of strategy, in considering how best we can pursue meaningful disruption, then the answer most surely is direct action. We have few other options: the legal system and accountability mechanisms are incredibly weak. In Britain, these arms sales appear[3] to already be in violation of the country's obligations under the Arms Trade Treaty (ATT) and its own strategic export licensing criteria and the government is happy to ignore unfavourable rulings in export-related court cases brought against it.[4] In addition to reducing the stringency of its weapons licensing *overall*, Britain has in the past even loosened its licensing *specifically* to expediate transfers of components to the US for Israel's US made weaponry. In the US, which supplies the vast majority of military equipment, vehicles, and munitions to Israel, the details of these transfers – such as quantity and type – are largely kept secret. Opaque licensing arrangements in most of Europe mean that the exact nature of transfers is hard to determine. The British, US, and NATO supplies are largely being flown from the RAF's base in Cyprus, but MPs have been blocked from raising questions about this.[5] What this means is that arms sales and transfers are largely insulated from democratic oversight, and that the millions protesting throughout these countries are not afforded the opportunity to challenge these licences and shipments in court.

There is clearly no appetite among the political class for critical assessment of the human rights concerns of these weapons sales and transfers. Given that no major political party in Britain or the US is willing to criticise Israel's actions, let alone express concerns about the human rights implications of Israel's use of British and US weaponry, activist groups and networks are increasingly taking the matter into their own hands the use of direct action strategies has, since October, accelerated under groups and coalitions led by members of trade unions, activists, or both. These campaigns are approaching Palestinian solidarity through a critical understanding of the West's role as a sponsor of the Israeli occupation. Targeting factories, offices, logistics and shipping, direct action solidarity in the West means recognising and opposing the part that our industries are playing in enabling this genocide.

This principle is what has always underpinned the work of Palestine Action, a direct-action network whose activists have spent three years occupying and blockading the premises of Israel-supplying weapons firms. For the most part, the group has worked to undermine Elbit Systems, Israel's largest arms company, which has been met with innumerable actions at its factories, offices, and also at the premises of its suppliers and partners and during their appearances at conferences and other events.

The basic principle is that, by allowing Elbit to manufacture drones in Leicester and Staffordshire, weapons sights in Kent, and parts for tanks in Tamworth, we ought to hold ourselves accountable for the fact that Israel deploys these weapons for genocidal purposes. Hundreds of actions have taken place, including dozens of multiple-days-long factory occupations, and thousands have been mobilised in actions or in support of actions. This consistent campaign of intensive action, and the risks taken and sacrifices made by committed activists, has already cost Elbit dearly. When Palestine Action launched, Elbit had ten sites in Britain. Two have now been closed permanently, and those still remaining have faced three years of constant disruption. Importantly, Britain's procurement relationship with Elbit has been damaged. The company has been deemed an inappropriate partner for British Ministry of Defence projects, and has been ejected from hundred-million-pound contracts as a result of Palestine Action sabotage.[6] The long-term, cumulative effect of disruption to Elbit's operations in Britain, therefore, is the jeopardising of its ability to embed itself in the country's military.

Activists have taken action against a growing list of weapons companies, including the likes of Leonardo, Thales and Rafael, as we seek to shut down all those complicit in Israel's arms trade. In recent weeks, our direct action has expanded dramatically to meet the urgency of the situation, though for over three years the primary purpose of the mobilisation has been to undermine Elbit Systems. This co-ordinated and deliberate strategy of direct action, with a clear and consistent target, has now commenced in the United States. Palestine Action US launched in October 2023 and is already undertaking mass action blockades and occupations to challenge Elbit's operations across its various sites. In Massachusetts, Vermont, Virginia, New Hampshire, and elsewhere, Elbit are now waking up to the reality that opposition to its activities is widespread, that its low profile is in jeopardy, and that it will be facing growing resistance in all of its host countries.

The reason Elbit is based in Britain, the US, the EU, and Australia is because there is clearly an appetite for its weaponry among these imperial Western powers. We can see how this works in Elbit's UAV Tactical Systems factory in Leicester, a site that has been breached, occupied, and blockaded by Palestine Action dozens of times. The factory, when it is operational, is used to ship military drones to Israel, to the value of £5m yearly, as well as to repackage and sell on these Israeli drone technologies back to the British military.[7] U-TacS' *Hermes* drones, notorious for the targeted killings and precision bombings that they enable against Gazans, have been turned into the 'Watchkeeper', designed for the Ministry of Defence, which has deployed it in Iraq and Afghanistan, and has also used it to prevent refugee crossings in the English Channel. Israel is not a customer of the *Watchkeeper* drone, and nor is Britain one of *Hermes*, yet parts are transferred between the countries. This is because it is essentially the same drone, and by repackaging the technology in this way Elbit can use its Leicester site to doubly profit by selling its custom drones to the MoD and its source material to Israel.

As a comrade has pointed out in *Ebb Magazine* previously,[8] the same intrusive and oppressive technologies of control, which secure the perimeter of the Gaza and render it an 'open-air prison', are deployed in the US, fortifying the illegal border wall with Mexico and facilitating the monitoring and surveillance of indigenous populations. In the months and years to come, the new weapons that Elbit and the Israeli military have been 'testing out' in this current onslaught will likely be entering European and US markets.[9]

Western powers therefore stand to benefit from this genocide, as their militaries are bolstered by Israel's murderous technologies, and their weapons manufacturing is stimulated by the increased demand from Israel. It is this abhorrent partnership, and Western profiteering from Palestinian deaths, that Palestine Action seeks to disrupt. Our governments are not passive supporters but are in fact active participants in Israel's campaign of ethnic cleansing. They have armed Israel for decades at an increasing rate, and have provided logistics support and equipment and personnel transfers throughout October and November 2023. Sunak's and Biden's failure to call for a ceasefire or to offer even the mildest criticism of Netanyahu's policies is not merely a matter of politics and personality. There are strategic and economic reasons for why our governments continue to offer their support to the occupation. The maintenance of imperial power in the region, and the reciprocal benefits for the military-technological industries of the West and Israel mean that we are in bed with the regime.

Those looking to resist Israel's violent settler-colonial project and Western complicity in it should consider this question first and foremost: how, with what, and from where are weapons being made for or transported to Israel from my country, and what can I do about it? Disrupting the arms industry in general, and Elbit Systems in particular, along with the shipment of its military products, should be the focus of an international effort by activists and trade unionists. Actions should follow on from words here, particularly when disruption to this industry has been requested by Palestinian trade unions themselves. In some parts of Europe, we have seen unions, specifically those of transport and freight workers, identifying the role that their industries play in arming Israel and acting accordingly to curtail this. At the end of October 2023, Belgian transport unions announced their refusal to load weapons shipments for Israel. The following week, port workers unions in Türkiye, Italy, and Greece jointly announced the same action, as did dock workers in Barcelona.

Others are lagging behind. In Britain, Canada, the US and Australia, opposition to Israel and its ongoing presence in those countries is being left to autonomous membership organisers while major unions neglect practical action. Union leaders have not necessarily considered how members may be inadvertently contributing through their work to Israeli settler-colonialism in Palestine. Unions including Unite, GMB, and Prospect hold recognition agreements with the defence and aerospace companies manufacturing weaponry for Israel, including the likes of Leonardo, Babcock, and BAE Systems. The RMT, rightly praised for adopting a strong verbal stance against Is-

rael's actions, has vowed to 'oppose' arms transfers to Israel, but without details of what this will entail, materially, in terms of whether there will be refusals to load Israel-bound weapons cargo.[10] In addition, it has not recalled those members that are currently working on Royal Fleet Auxiliary Ships stationed to support the onslaught on Gaza. Statements and appearances at rallies do not undo the fact that there is complicity by association through involvement in militaries and military industries.

This means that labour movement activity in Britain to address the complicity of businesses and industries in the Israeli occupation has largely been consolidated among self-organising union members – including, recently, instances of mass action factory blockades under the banner *Workers for a Free Palestine*. This self-organising, particularly when it critically engages with the relevant industries and challenges business activity, is a noteworthy development, and labour movement bureaucracies should take heed of their members' will for action. The same is true elsewhere. In Australia, the Australian Council of Trade Unions' calls for a ceasefire are dampened by its lack of action in relation to weapons shipments; instead, direct action under the 'Unionists for Palestine' banner has stopped, or attempted to stop, Israeli cargo ships from docking. This is the case, too, in the US, where the Palestinians' calls for the cessation of arms to Israel has been answered by direct action groups convening to blockade ports, notably on the West Coast, while others organise to disrupt factory operations – with actions not only by Palestine Action US, but also by activist coalitions such as that which blockaded Boeing in Missouri.[11]

There ought to be coordinated, global efforts to undermine Israel's arms imports and exports, using direct action by means of sabotage, blockade, occupation, or whatever other action might be necessary. We also need to keep building international networks and gathering intelligence on companies arming Israel, including details of their products and their sites. The company that provides 85% of Israel's drones, all of its small calibre-munitions, vast ranges of bombs, sights, surveillance gear, communications (and innumerable other things), and which is already subject to intensive anti-occupation mobilisation across different continents, seems like the best place to start. Elbit Systems ought to be held responsible for its products' integral role in genocide and occupation, and we ought to hold ourselves accountable for its continuing presence in our countries.

In the process of disrupting this industry in Britain, hundreds have been arrested, some of them then handed draconian charges and sometimes lengthy, tiresome prosecutions. Comrades in the US have already been arrested in considerable numbers, some held without charge or bail, while in Britain a number of activists have spent time in prison and more are threatened with that possibility. It is not just the British and US governments that are interested in locking up those standing against Elbit; Israel has sought to exert its own influence on the prosecution of Palestine Action activists.[12]

Nevertheless, direct action is taken in the knowledge that Elbit is the guilty party. And given the failure of legalistic mechanisms to prevent weapons sales to Israel, direct action is the only way to restrict Elbit's participation in Israel's crimes. It is the only way to protect lives and make Elbit bear responsibility for its part in this colonial violence. Activists in Britain have in fact successfully argued this in court, and have been acquitted on the basis that their actions were necessary interventions to preserve life and protect property in Gaza.[13] That people can be arrested, harassed by the state and made to endure massively disproportionate prosecutions is partly to be expected – particularly given that, by exposing and disrupting the West's criminal weapons industry, these activists are also bringing to light the despicable involvement of our own governments in Israel's ethnic cleansing. But this state repression is made more endurable when your conscientious, direct action has offered an *actual* impediment to the operations of weapons companies. Ultimately, working to undermine this imperial machinery offers the best hope for any individual wanting to contribute to Palestinian's struggle against occupation. As Workers in Palestine made clear, '[t]he time for action is now – Palestinian lives hang in the balance'.

Liam Doherty is an activist with Palestine Action, @pal_action.

References

1   'Palestinian Trade Unions Call for an End to Arming Israel', MERIP, 2023.
2   'Netherlands providing Israel with F-35 fighter jet parts despite war crime concerns', NL Times, 2023.
3   Charles Schulz, 'Trading in trauma: do United Kingdom arms exports to Israel violate the Arms Trade Treaty and other arms control regulations?', Action on Armed Violence, 2023.
4   Dan Sabbagh, 'Truss admits UK broke ban on Saudi arms sales three times', The Guardian, 2019.
5   Matt Kennard and Mark Curtis, 'UK Government Blocks MP Questions about Gaza-Related Activity at its Cyprus Base', Declassified, 2023.
6   Huda Ammori, 'Elbit's contract losses prove that economic sabotage works', The New Arab, 2022.
7   'UK Elbit factory protest enters 87th day', MEMO, 2023.
8   Dante, 'Unravelling the Paper Tiger: Palestine Action's Siege', Ebb Magazine, 2023.
9   'Israel tests new Iron Sting bomb in Gaza', MEMO, 2023.
10   RMT Union, 'Head Office Circular No: NP/184/23', 2023.
11   Monica Obradovic, 'Activists Block Entrances to St. Charles Boeing Plant', Riverfront Times, 2023.
12   Haroon Siddique, 'Israeli embassy officials attempted to influence UK court cases, documents suggest', The Guardian, 2023.
13   'Pro-Palestine activist acquitted of criminal damage charge against supplier of materials for Israel fighter jets', MEMO, 2023.

What I Have to Do
Dáithí Bowen

They bombed a hospital. This I know.
What I have to do.[1]
I know the casualties number in the hundreds, out of total death toll of thousands, and will keep
rising until the Palestinians are / dead / gone / cleansed.
White horse left alone. What I have to do.
I know the media lies, and that if they do not have lies to repeat, then they will have apologies and reasons and excuses.
Blood on their hands. What I have to do.
I know that I know very little of airstrikes and dust in my mouth and shattered eardrums and split
skulls and children's bodies in parts.
Death at full speed. Senses not yet deranged. What I have to do.
I know that metaphors can't survive in an open air prison, and that any attempt to write
poetry after Gaza is just barbarism.
Stop writing. What I have to do.
I know that cultural resistance means nothing when poets can be murdered and the Freedom Theatre can be bulldozed and Zakaria Zubeidi is still in prison.
Stop writing. What I have to do.
I know I live in the belly of the beast / Balfour / British complicity a century old.
Drop everything. Get out and go. What I have to do.
I know that Elbit Systems has eight factories in the UK, has a network of partners and supply chains to make 50 further sites. I know Rafael owns a Newcastle factory for armoured vehicles and Thales sinks its talons into Scotland.
Belly of the beast. What I have to do.
I know these places are not in some land separated by distance and mass media, but they are
here, and they can be broken and dismantled and destroyed.
The weaving frame can be smashed. What I have to do.
I know that none of us are free till Palestine is free, that the company which made Grenfell's cladding makes the materials for fighter jets and helicopters in israel, and that the Watchkeeper drone is used in Palestine and on the British borders.
None of us are free till all of us are free. What I have to do.
I know that despite it all our words can be made flesh, and the hydra's head can be severed. A coin older than the Zionist entity dangles on my chest to remind me of the eternal oscillation of human fortunes, and that someday the last will be first.
By any means necessary. What I have to do.

Dáithí Bowen is a British poet of Irish heritage. Their writing includes essays and poetry pamphlets such as Hooligan Communism & Other Poems, Homo Sacer, *and 32* Stars in a Wretched Sky.

References

1   This refrain is taken from the novel *Q* by Luther Blissett, an Italian writing collective now known as Wu Ming. The poem's penultimate line is a détournement of another line from *Q*: 'The coin of the kingdom of the mad dangles on my chest to remind me of the eternal oscillation of human fortunes.'

'A Bond of the Same Nature': Cartographies of Affiliation in the Global South

Suleiman Hodali

Palestine and 'the Common Struggle' of Third World Solidarity

A delegation of Palestinian representatives delivered their speech to the international audience meeting in Gaza from December 9-11, 1961, in the name of the Arab Palestinian people:

> We welcome you and thank you for convening the Executive Committee of the Afro-Asian Peoples Solidarity Conference in this part of our stolen homeland, Palestine. This generous action portrays the meaning of feelings of both African and Asian peoples, their understanding of the extent of oppression which we suffer from, their determination to stand by us for the consolidation of our just struggle in the different spheres.[1]

From all corners of Africa and Asia – belonging to a transcontinental bloc of formerly and currently colonised nations which, during the cold war era, became known as the Third World – over thirty delegations and observers assembled at this crossroads between both continents to attend the Executive Committee of the Afro-Asian Peoples' Solidarity Organisation (AAPSO).[2] The meeting facilitated a unique conjunction of interlocutors from diverse formations of lo-

calised struggle and national politics. And in the eyes of the Palestinian host delegation, like Che Guevara's 1959 visit to Gaza, the Executive Committee's decision to assemble in Gaza alone embodied a gesture of unequivocal support by African and Asian peoples to advance their own just struggle against the continual violations of Zionism's settler-colonial violence inflicted on native life in Palestine.

The 1961 Gaza meeting marks a decisive moment in the symbolic identification between Palestine's spatial centrality as a bridge between Africa and Asia, and its historical and moral centrality to the formation of an emergent Afro-Asian consciousness. Among the conference participants present in Gaza were figures like Osendé Afana, the militant Marxist economist of Cameroon, as well as Mehdi Ben Barka, the socialist activist and anti-monarchist exile from Morocco – both of whom, just a few years later, would be assassinated and disappeared by the repressive forces of imperialism against which they had struggled. In Gaza, young communist activists like Wera Ambitho – secretary of the anti-colonial Kenya Office in Cairo – found proximity to distinguished critical theorists like Yoshitaro Hirano – founder of the Marxist tradition in Japan – as well as experienced organisers like the long-time Communist Party of India leader and World Peace Council activist, Romesh Chandra. Bureaucratic statesmen of the arts and letters, like Han Sorya – the celebrated author, Korean Writers' Union head, and DPRK Minister of Education and Culture – and the Russian playwright and Soviet Writers Union secretary, Anatoly Sofronov, in Gaza found analogue resonances among such figures as Zia al-Din Tabataba'i, former Prime Minister of Iran, and cosmopolitan diplomats from China, like Liao Chengzhi and Burhan Shahidi.

For the Palestinian host delegation, the particular histories which belonged to these respective visiting delegations reflected a diverse set of triumphs, lessons, and tactics of resistance, the sum of which formed a Third World epistemology of anti-colonialism – a set of theories and practices for resistance against imperialism upon which to model their own struggles. And to this diverse, multi-national audience, the Palestinian delegation's speech affirmed the imbricated relationship of their own anti-imperialist struggle to those before them, both literally and historically:

> Your victories are a prelude to ours and to all peoples fighting for their freedom and dignity. The Afro-Asian Solidarity Movement is not an emotional one, but a historical movement, evolving with the days, drawing its experiences from the common struggle, and drawing its plans from the hopes to which our people aspire for a free and dignified life.

> Friends, you have heard much about the Palestinian cause from friends and enemies, but today you will witness our reality, to which Anglo-American and French, Zionist conspiracies has led us. No doubt knowledge of the pains and hopes of peoples is [the] best way for the establishment of a just peace to hover over humanity.[3]

The sympathetic identification with Palestine – ascribed to the 'meaning of feelings of both African and Asian peoples' – is nev-ertheless 'not an emotional one', but determined instead by an acknowledgment of the historical affinities between their pasts and futures. Palestinians thus carved their own position within a broader assemblage of Third World consciousness, 'drawing its experiences from the common struggle, and drawing its plans from the hopes to which our people aspire for a free and dignified life'.

Affirmations of Palestinian self-identification with the pasts and futures of African, Asian, and Latin American struggles reveal a recurrent *affiliative* mode of national representation – whereby Palestinians signify their own historical experience in figurative modes of comparative legibility – recognising their own among disparate global struggles against settler-colonialism and imperialism. 'We take this opportunity,' the 1961 Palestinian delegation in Gaza continued in its address, 'to hail the martyrs of freedom who fell on the battlefield of duty, as the martyrs, [Patrice] Lumumba, and [Félix-Roland] Moumié as well as all freemen who are fighting behind the prison bars as [Ahmed] Ben Bella and his comrades. They are torchlights lighting the road of freedom and honour'.[4] In the betrayal of Lumumba's independence by UN liaisons with the imperial designs of American and Belgian forces, and the repression of Algerian resistance by French imperialism, Palestinians recognised their own commonalities in the dominative systems of colonial rule against which they struggled.

But more than provincially-bound struggles signifying comparative analogues to Palestinian resistance against Zionist settler-colonialism - as an ethno-supremacist state sustained by the United States' support - the Palestinian delegation's address insisted that the existence of Israel also presented a direct threat to the national sovereignty of African and Asian nations, since:

> Colonialism helped as well to let Israel infiltrate ... the markets of Africa and Asia, with the purpose of using it as a tool and screen for colonialist capital monopolies in the markets of the two continents.

You are no doubt aware of the similar manoeuvres that have been employed in Palestine, and through which colonialism endeavours to dominate Algeria, Angola, the Congo and South Africa, by mobilising minorities in these countries to play with the destiny of the peoples. All colonialist attempts to repress these peoples and obstruct their unity and liberation, have no other aim than to set new strong posts, bridges and other agents, in different parts of Africa to be complementary parts to the first imperialist base established in Arab Palestine.[5]

While colonial regimes continued to persist across Africa even after the formal age of empire had come to a close, the establishment of a settler-colonial state in Palestine during the age of decolonisation signalled the veritable reformulation of Western imperialism by any other name. Palestinians thus appealed to those sovereign states recently 'releas[ed] from the fetters of colonialism' to 'fulfil their responsibility towards the cause of freedom and justice'.

Such a responsibility grounded Third World solidarity in the values of a humanist discourse which transcended the racialised limits of a humanism wielded by Western liberalism to rationalise its colonial enterprise in the previous century:

The upsurge of Afro-Asian peoples is both old and new, new because these peoples are newly liberated from colonialist domination, and old because [anti-colonial resistance is] a defence of human values ever since the dawn of history. We all hope for just Peace, and the Afro-Asian peoples have a great responsibility towards humanity which nearly is going to land itself in the plot of destruction, after development of destructive weapons and its well-designed tactics to do away with the freedom of man. May our movement prevent storms that may hit humanity from the dangers of colonialism against the liberation of peoples fighting for their liberty, and against the liberation of the peoples of colonised

countries from their colonial rulers.[6]

In declaring the formation of 'our movement,' the anti-colonial struggle for Palestinian liberation became infused with a markedly global character, and the question of Palestine was reified as a definitive cause for an emergent Third World consciousness.

The generous action of convening in Gaza to *witness* their reality reflects an active effort by the visiting Executive Committee to further their '*understanding* of the extent of oppression from which [Palestinians] suffer,' so as to better serve as determined advocates for their struggle in the realm of different cultural and political spheres. To bear witness in Gaza is thus inexorably to develop a direct *knowledge* of Palestinians' pains and hopes – and an intimate awareness with the material conditions against which to pursue the 'establishment of a just peace.'

Established in 1957 at the first Afro-Asian Peoples' Solidarity Conference in Cairo (December 26, 1957-January 1, 1958), AAPSO explicitly affirmed its organisational contours around the spirit of Third World solidarity inaugurated by the Bandung Conference of April 1955. The twenty-nine African and Asian states represented at Bandung established their commonalities as recently decolonised nation-states within an international order shaped by the bi-polarised logic of the cold war. The question of Palestine received considerable attention at Bandung where it was championed with great urgency by representatives from Egypt, Syria, and China – despite attempts by Indian and Burmese delegates to sideline the issue from discussions. Indeed, prior to the conference, at the suggestion Israel would be invited to participate in its proceedings, Arab representatives threatened to boycott the meeting. The limits of Bandung were thus made legible by the conference's occlusion of self-representation for African and Asian nations still struggling directly under repressive forms of imperial domination. And future formations for cooperative exchange between African and Asian nations[7] (such as that represented by AAPSO) were motivated by political and cultural initiatives that centred their solidarity around mutual support for *ongoing* struggles against colonialism – which found Palestine imbricated with such places as Algeria, Congo, Korea, Rhodesia, South Africa, and Vietnam, among others.

Organised with Soviet support through the initiative of Egyptian president Gamal Abdel Nasser in the aftermath of the Suez Crisis, the first Afro-Asian People's Solidarity Conference in 1957 made greater strides than its progenitor at Bandung to underscore the persistence of colonial exploitation and dispossession across Africa and Asia in the so-called age of decolonisation. In addition to adopting the Bandung Conference's ten principles for peaceful co-existence – which entrusted the post-WWII order of international law based on the Charter of the United Nations – AAPSO's inaugural 1957 conference in Cairo also adopted political resolutions in the spirit of Bandung which went further than that paradigmatic 1955 event to underline the importance of support for *current* struggles against colonialism as the basis for cultivating Third World solidarity.

Some of these resolutions adopted at the 1957 Conference condemned, respectively: the apartheid system of racial discrimination in South Africa; the French republic's 'colonial war [aimed] at the extermination of the Algerian people'; and the state of Israel, originally established in clear defiance of the Rights of Man,' as a 'base of imperialism which threatens the progress and security of all the Middle East, and [...] its aggressive policy which is a threat to world peace'. This latter resolution, based on a report submitted by the Palestine Delegation, radically redressed Bandung's muted position on the topic, which deferred to 'the implementation of the United Nations decisions on Palestine' to achieve a 'peaceful settlement of the Palestine question'.

Whereas Bandung's deference to the UN tacitly recognised the legitimacy of Israel's acceptance in an international world order, the 1957 resolution on Palestine adopted by AAPSO implicitly challenged such premises. The report upon which the resolution was based chronicled the history of Zionism's arrival in Palestine as a handmaiden of British colonialism, and – following the establishment of Israel – its inheritance by the US to sustain an effective garrison state through which to leverage American imperial interests in the region. Future resolutions adopted at subsequent AAPSO conferences continued to develop more nuanced analyses of the threat posed by Israel – not only to Palestinians living under its repressive military occupation, or as refugees banished without return to their homes, but – as a tool of American imperialism, to the independence of African and Asian nations, in general terms.

And it was at the 1961 meeting in Gaza that AAPSO began to firmly problematise the legitimacy of Israel's existence according to the accepted basis of international law. The Executive Committee adopted a resolution proclaiming 'that Palestine is an Arab territory and that the propping up of Israel in this Arab territory on the dead bodies of its people is an illegal action that violates the principles of international law, human rights and the United Nations Charter'. Thus, the resolution continued:

> Israel is an aggressive entity propped up by imperialism to be used in striking and menacing national liberation movements in the Middle East area, infiltrating to the other parts of Asia and Africa and that Israel is a tool in the hand of neo-colonialism, as proved by events and therefore the Committee draws the attention of all Afro-Asian peoples to the reality of this colonialist tool and its danger to World Peace.

> The Committee supports Arab rights in Palestine and their rightful cause to liberate their homeland and return to it and asks all Afro-Asian peoples to do the same.[8]

While the 1961 Executive Committee meeting in Gaza confirmed 'all the resolutions adopted concerning Palestine in all the past Afro-Asian Conferences convened in Cairo,

Conakry, Casablanca and Bandung,' it also signalled a markedly emphatic recognition of Israel's functional logic as a vassal state strategically located at the crossroads of Africa and Asia to serve the advancement of US imperial interests between both continents.

Such declarations and resolutions adopted by AAPSO and other organisations highlight the diplomatic processes by which Palestine became enshrined as a central cause in the cultivation of a Third World consciousness. Palestinian steadfastness against colonial erasures and imperial domination increasingly emblematised the humanist struggle for liberation which buttressed Third World solidarity. What's more, the inclusion of Palestinian self-representation among the proceedings of events convened by such bodies as AAPSO, OSPAAAL (Organisation of Solidarity with the People of Asia, Africa and Latin America), the Conference of Independent African States, the All-African People's Conference, and the Pan African Cultural Festival throughout the 1960s likewise nourished the political and cultural development of a Palestinian national consciousness – increasingly articulated in reflexive terms of identification with the symbols and histories of comparative struggles against colonialism from across the Third World.

To trace, among these transcontinental encounters and exchanges, Palestine's gradual entrenchment as a vanguard of Third World struggles also reveals how the lineages of Bandung endured and matured. The growing participation of Palestinian representatives among such meetings thus betrays the global formations of Palestinian self-determination after 1948.

In their description of the '[new] upsurge of Afro-Asian peoples', unified by a shared commitment to 'a defence of human values' the Palestinian delegation echoes the closing of Franz Fanon's *Wretched of the Earth*, first published that same year, which enjoined that, 'for humanity, comrades, we must turn over a new leaf, we must work out new concepts, and try to set afoot a new man'. In de-

claring the shared responsibility towards humanity which underlines the movement, the anti-colonial struggle for Palestinian liberation became inscribed with a markedly global character, and the question of Palestine reified as an exemplary cause in the broader assemblage of Third World solidarity.

New Humanisms and the Universalism of Third World Poetics

At a July 1966 Emergency Meeting of the Afro-Asian Writers' Conference in Beijing, the intensity of Palestinians' sympathetic affiliations with anti-imperial struggles in the global South became palpable in the figure of Palestinian writer and revolutionary, Ghassan Kanafani. As one biographer notes:

> A North Vietnamese writer, after reading his speech, distributed to the other members of the congress shrapnel souvenirs from the remains of an American plane which had been shot down a week before; Kanafani was immensely touched by this episode. When his turn to speak came he did not read his prepared speech. Instead he said he had nothing to offer in the way his North Vietnamese colleague had, but promised to do so at the next conference. Then he sat down and burst into tears.[9]

Convened in response to splittist threats from growing Sino-Soviet tensions in the Afro-Asian Writers Bureau, the Emergency Meeting was organised by the Chinese government to reaffirm its commitment to solidarity with struggles of the Third World. Among the many resolutions passed in support of anti-colonial struggles across Africa and Asia, the 'Resolution on Palestine' adopted by the 1966 Emergency Meeting emphatically pronounced its commitment to Palestinian self-determination by calling for 'an economic and cultural boycott of Israel and that Israel be ousted from international organisations', and 'be completely liquidated'.

The following year, at the Soviet-sponsored Third Afro-Asian Writers Conference in Beirut, Kanafani once again served as a Palestinian delegate where he delivered a lecture on 'Resistance Literature in Palestine' – published the following year in *Afro-Asian Writings*, a quarterly publication of the Permanent Bureau of Afro-Asian Writers. From the particular experience of Palestinian citizens of Israel who, as a minority in their homeland, lived under a repressive military occupation from 1948-1967, Kanafani derives a theory of resistance literature that serves as a universal model for a Third World humanism – a popular culture and poetics formed in dialectic opposition to the ontologies of colonialism's epistemological dominations and erasures. Estranged from the surrounding Arab world, and subject to Israel's repressive cultural siege against native education and self-representation – the Palestinian writer under colonial rule exemplified, for Kanafani, the paradigm of a critical consciousness shaped by an oppositional relationship to colonial forms of knowledge production and an attendant epistemic violence of negation and denial. 'After the fall of Palestine in 1948', Kanafani explained:

> popular literature remained the outlet through which the oppressed people expressed their anguish. It seems that when weddings in Galilee turned into demonstrations through the words of popular bards and poets, the Zionist occupation forces opened fire on the demonstrators. The Zionist authorities were later forced to submit a large number of 'popular reciters' to the military governor and to impose strict control on their movements. Nevertheless, words proved to be more effective than fire and capable of breaking the siege. In May 1958, Arab demonstrators clashed with the enemy police, and several people were killed in the fight. Shoulder to shoulder, the demonstrators rushed into the police lines, broke their ranks, and pushed them down the road. With this incident a new song was born and spread out in Galilee.[10]

In recognising the occasional force of resistance literature, Kanafani underlines the social history of written cultures, giving prominence to the verbal chants, songs, and orations which first materialise from the scenes of popular struggle. By the 1960s, as Maha Nassar's work has shown, Palestinian poets in Israel represented their experience with local conditions of colonialism in terms of global struggles from the Congo to Vietnam. Mahmoud Darwish, Kanafani points out, 'wrote a collection of poems entitled *Birds Without Wings* about the African Liberation struggle, in which his intent cannot be mistaken by the reader'.[11]

The 1967 Resolution on Palestine adopted at the Third Afro-Asian Writers Conference in Beirut – where Kanafani had lived in exile since 1960 – positions the figure of the Palestinian writer under Zionist military rule as the paradigm for a transnational figure of the 'Afro-Asian writer'.[12]

The first five points of the 1967 resolution – adopted just months before the June War which hastened Israel's ongoing occupation of the West Bank, Gaza, and the Golan Heights – delineate Israel's role as a 'bridge-head of a neo-colonialism.' And the following points extend a recognition of the role that language and culture hold as weapons of resistance with which to directly challenge the epistemic violence of colonialism. Appealing to 'all progressive writers in the world to stand in the face of the wide cultural conspiracy launched by the Zionist movement through writers who have betrayed the honour of the written word in order to serve interests that are contradictory to the rudiments of truth and History', the Resolution proffers an injunction, no doubt invoked by Kanafani, 'to take action, as strongly as possible, in order to stem that misleading cultural aggression through a quest for truth and an appeal to consolidate it'.

Two years after he and his young niece Lamis were assassinated in Beirut by the Mossad,[13] Kanafani was announced as a posthumous recipient of the 1974 Lotus Prize for Afro-Asian Literature. That same year, an essay by the Egyptian literary scholar Ezzedine Ismail was published in *Lotus* magazine[14] and built on Kanafani's previous theorisations on the figure of the 'Afro-Asian writer'. In 'Afro-Asian Literature: Its Nature and the Role It plays Against Imperialist Aggression, Racial Discrimination, and Zionism', Ismail points to the political role of the Afro-Asian writer as a figure embedded in the particular circumstances of specific national exigencies but who simultaneously inhabits a transnational purview of liberation informed by commitment to universal principles. Inexorably circumscribed by local conditions of repression enabled through broader, global systems of economic and military domination:

> The Afro-Asian writer is by no means a spectator, either with regard to his own people or the peoples of the two continents. He is bound to his people with the ties which bind the citizen to his nationality and, at the same time, he is bound to all the peoples of the two continents with a bond of the same nature. 'Afro-Asianism' has become, for him, a wider and more comprehensive nationality.[15]

'With a bond of the same nature', the Afro-Asian writer inherits its *filial* attachments to formations of national consciousness while simultaneously apprehending a set of universal principles derived from a global history of anti-colonialism. For the Afro-Asian writer, sites of native familiarity thus become inscribed with relational, *affiliative* significations to other geographies upon which similar systems of imperial domination and colonial violence have been visited. As a site in which Zionist settler-colonialism and American imperialism have been consolidated, to Ismail, Palestine represents a core paradigm of identification for all valences of Third World struggle:

> Contemporary Arabic literature all over the Arab world, and not in Palestine alone, has taken the cause of Palestine and the Palestinian people to its heart and made it its main preoccupation, not only because Palestine is part of the Arab world, but also because Zionism represents the imperialist ideology that

is destructive to peoples and to humanity and has expansionist plans not only for the Middle East, but for Asia and Africa. It is the duty of the writers of Asia and Africa to realise this fact and to shoulder their responsibility against that new colonialist octopus. Zionism in the Middle East is not different in any way from racial discrimination in South Africa, colonialism in the Portuguese colonies or the military commercial complex that is exploiting and victimising the Asiatic countries.[16]

Ismail's emphasis on the domain of writing and literature as a front in the warfare of resistance against imperialist ideology also extends the lessons of Kanafani's 1968 critical study on Palestinian cultural production *Resistance Literature in Occupied Palestine: 1948-1967*. There, Kanafani includes selections of Palestinian literature characteristic of resistance literature, among which appear several poems by the Palestinian poet, Samih al-Qassim. Alongside poems dedicated to the Vietcong and to Fidel Castro, al-Qassim's poem 'To Paul Robeson' demonstrates how Palestinian articulations of resistance looked to struggles from across the Third World – and indeed, within the interior of the American metropole – as a symbolic landscape of racialised stratification:

> From the ends of the world
> Your singing flows in my house
> And flutters in my heart.
> An exiled brown bird
> From the farthest ends of the world
> Your singing flows in my house.
> Oh, the deepest voice
> Your singing flows in my house
> Oh, the farthest sign on the path
> Oh, the scandalous injustice of man against man
> From the farthest ends of the world:
> 'For God's sake, take my mother home
> So that she does not witness my death.'
> And wander into my eyes
> Ghosts of the Ku Klux Klan
> Having fun with your crucifixion in the field

Having fun with my crucifixion in the field
I woke up to the sound of a drum
Faith returns to my heart![17]

Flowing from the 'farthest ends of the world' into the domestic spaces of interiority, al-Qassim's poetic speaker identifies Robeson as a consummate figure of resistance to the injustices of racial discrimination replicated between the United States and Israel and the common struggle against elimination is equally ascribed to a desire for a future of freedom and liberation. The cartographic imagination of the Third World has been supplanted by that identified with the global South, but what remains constant in Palestine's current global moment is a heritage of solidarity.

As the 1969 address of the Palestine Liberation Organisation to the Pan African Culture Festival in Algiers declared:

We therefore look to all the revolutionaries in Africa to stand with us, with the cause of freedom in Palestine as they stand with the cause of freedom in Africa. As the cause of freedom is one and indivisible.

[We] believe that the cause of freedom is one and the cause of Revolution is one all over the world. As we feel responsibility towards all revolutionaries, we decided to extend our absolute unlimited and unreserved support to all those who carry arms fighting for the cause of liberty everywhere, especially in Africa which suffers in its struggle for human existence on the homeland.

[We] intend to take a leading role in the revolutionary movement … as a militant pioneer in Palestine would intercede with all militant pioneers in Africa who intend to fight for liberty anywhere in the world that suffers from oppression, privation, racism, colonialism and neo-colonialism.

This is not political propaganda. It is a pledge [to which Palestine] clings with full understanding, to its responsibility towards the map of world Revolution.[18]

Suleiman Hodali is a writer and researcher in Los Angeles, where he is completing a PhD in comparative literature. His recent work has appeared in Studies in Romanticism.

References

1   'Supplement on the Afro-Asian People's Solidarity Executive Committee Gaza from 9th to 11th December 1961', *Afro-Asian Bulletin*, No. 1 (Supplement) Vol. IV Jan./Feb. 1962, 45.

2   Participating Delegates included Algeria, Cameroon, Congo, China, Guinea, India, Iran, Iraq, Indonesia, Kenya, Japan, North Korea, Lebanon, Morocco, Mongolia, Southern Rhodesia, South West Africa, Tunisia, Uganda, United Arab Republic, U.S.S.R, Vietnam, and Yemen, as well as Observer participants representing Palestine, Basutoland, Nigeria, North Rhodesia, Oman, Ruanda-Urundi, Zanzibar, the World Peace Council, and Afro-Asian Lawyers.

3   'Supplement on the Afro-Asian People's Solidarity Executive Committee Gaza from 9th to 11th December 1961', 45.

4   'Supplement on the Afro-Asian People's Solidarity Executive Committee Gaza from 9th to 11th December 1961', 46.

5   'Supplement on the Afro-Asian People's Solidarity Executive Committee Gaza from 9th to 11th December 1961', 46.

6   'Supplement on the Afro-Asian People's Solidarity Executive Committee Gaza from 9th to 11th December 1961', 46.

7   And, beginning with the 1966 Tricontinental Conference in Havana, Cuba, between African, Asian, and Latin American nations.

8   'Supplement on the Afro-Asian People's Solidarity Executive Committee Gaza from 9th to 11th December 1961', 25.

9   See Stefan Wild's *Ghassan Kanafani: The Life of a Palestinian* (1975), 17. My thanks to Esmat Elhalaby who shared this anecdote with me many years ago.

10   Ghassan Kanafani, 'Resistance Literature in Palestine', *Afro-Asian Writings* (nos. 2-3, Summer

1968), 66.

11   Ghassan Kanafani, 'Resistance Literature in Palestine', 71.

12   From the Third Afro-Asian Writers' Conference, March 25-30, 1967:

Resolution on Palestine

1) Considers the Zionist movement as colonialist by nature, expansionist in its aims, racist in its structure, fascist in the means it is using;

2) Considers Israel as an imperialist base and a docile tool used for aggressive purposes against Arab states in order to delay their progress towards unity and socialism, and as a bridge-head which neo-colonialism relies on in order to maintain its influence over African and Asian states;

3) Views the aggressive Israeli presence in Palestine as artificial, usurping and demographically imperialist, resorting to violent means and consequently considers the liquidation of this presence as a liberatory and urgent task;

4) Considers that a revolutionary solution to the problems of the Arab Nation, i.e., the liquidation of the reactionary and colonialist regimes, economic emancipation and progress, is primarily bound to the liquidation of Israel as a base intended to maintain backwardness in that region;

5) Views the Israeli presence as a fascist and racist system, in terms of a setback to civilisation directed against human progress;

6) Appeals to Afro-Asian Writers, and to all progressive writers in the world, to stand in the face of the wide cultural conspiracy launched by the Zionist movement through writers who have betrayed the honour of the written word in order to serve interests that are contradictory to the rudiments of truth and History, and to take action, as strongly as possible, in order to stem that misleading cultural aggression through a quest for truth and an appeal to consolidate it.

7) Denounces the heavy cultural siege laid by Israel on one quarter of a million Arabs living in occupied territory under a hateful racial oppression in their own land.

8) Hails Palestinian Arab Writers living in oc-cupied Palestine under terrorist rule, for their valiant stand in defence of the rights of the Palestinian people to liberate their country, and denounces the continuous oppression to which they are subjected at the hands of the occupational forces.

9) Hails progressive writers from Asia, Africa and the rest of the world who have, through their consciousness and courage, stood up to Zionist falsehoods and exposed them; and those who have, through their honourable and responsible pens, considerably reinforced the cause of the Palestinian people in their struggle for self-determination.

10) Considers the support given by the writers of Africa and Asia to the people of Palestine in their struggle for the liberation of their territory as an integral part of the support given to liberation in the world.

11) Supports the Palestine Liberation Organisation which leads the struggle of the Palestinian Arab people to liberate Palestine and to regain their usurped homeland by any means.

13   Louis Allday, 'A Race Against Time: The life and death of Ghassan Kanafani', *Mondoweiss*, 2023.

14   Beginning in the late 1960s, the flagship literary and cultural publication of the Afro-Asian Writers Bureau.

15   Ezzedine Ismail, 'Afro-Asian Literature: Its Nature and the Role it Plays Against Imperialist Aggression, Racial Discrimination, and Zionism', *Lotus: Afro-Asian Writings* 20 (1974), 41. Thank you to Sara Hussein for sharing this text with me, in addition to other AAPSO-related publications on the histories of Afro-Arab solidarity.

16   Ezzedine Ismail, 'Afro-Asian Literature: Its Nature and the Role it Plays Against Imperialist Aggression, Racial Discrimination, and Zionism', 58.

17   Samih al-Qassim 'To Paul Robeson' in Ghassan Kanafani, *Adab al-muqawamah fi Filastin al-muhtallah, 1948-1966* (Manshurat al-Rimal, 2015), 165-6 (my translation).

18   'Al-Fateh's communique at the 1969 Festival of Pan-African Culture', *Black Agenda Report*, 2023.

The Cause of Anti-Colonialism and Liberation is One: Fayez Sayegh's Zionist Colonialism in Palestine

Louis Allday

Zionism is a form of racism and racial discrimination.
– United Nations General Assembly Resolution 3379, 10 November 1975

The Syrian-Palestinian academic and diplomat, Fayez Sayegh (1922-1980), a delegate of Kuwait's Mission to the UN in the mid-1970s, was the principal author of the landmark resolution quoted above. Much to the chagrin of the US, whose representative described it as a "great evil ... loosed upon the world", the resolution was sponsored by the Arab states, and strongly supported by the Soviet Union and a large swathe of the newly independent states of the Global South.[1] Sixteen years later, Israel refused to participate in the Madrid Conference without its abrogation. With the opposing influence of the Soviet bloc gone, the US then exerted all its influence to ensure the resolution was repealed.[2] It remains the only UN General Assembly resolution to meet such a fate. Although short lived, it had served as global recognition of a position that Sayegh and his colleagues advocated for tirelessly over the preceding decades – one which had already been endorsed by a number of non-Western international organisations including the Non-Aligned Movement and the Organisation of African Unity.

A vital institution in this effort was the PLO's Palestine Research Center (PRC) in Beirut, as established by Sayegh in 1965. In its heyday, a who's who of Palestinian cultural and intellectual figures including Ghassan Kanafani, Mahmoud Darwish, Isma'il Shammout and Fayez's younger brother, Anis, worked for or contributed to the centre. Over almost two decades, it released more than four hundred publications about the Palestinian cause in multiple languages including Arabic, English, French, Spanish and even Esperanto.[3] This literature was distributed globally and was used in efforts to garner international support for Palestine. Organisations such as the Student Nonviolent Coordinating Committee (SNCC) released statements of solidarity with the Palestinians that were informed directly by PRC publications.[4] The Centre's work was brought to a halt following Israel's invasion of Lebanon in 1982. During the subsequent occupation, its archive and library were looted by Israeli troops[5] and a bombing gutted its Beirut headquarters, killing twenty people and injuring dozens more – many of them staff members.[6] These attacks were part of a broader Israeli assault in which its forces 'wiped out most of the Palestinian educational and cultural institutions they could get their hands on'.[7]

The first monograph released by the PRC, Sayegh's *Zionist Colonialism in Palestine* in 1965, is a concise and powerful study of the origins, character and strategies of the Zionist movement. It epitomises the stirring and informative literature the Centre excelled at producing. Given the clarity of Sayegh's analysis and the prescience of his conclusions, the book remains strikingly relevant more than fifty years since it was written. Contrary to the liberal-Zionist myth that Zionism began as a noble cause, but has been corrupted and dragged rightwards since 1967, Sayegh explains how Zionism was a colonialist and racist enterprise from its inception.[8] The present climate – in which there is an ongoing campaign by the US and Israeli governments (and affiliated Zionist pressure groups) to conflate anti-Zionism with anti-Semitism and, therefore, delegitimise opposition to Israel, makes the book's arguments all the more pertinent.

In his youth, Sayegh was a prominent member of the Syrian Social Nationalist Party but left after disagreements with its founder, Antoun Saadeh. He went on to complete a PhD on Existential Philosophy at Georgetown University, before holding a number of academic and diplomatic positions, mainly in the US. Surprisingly unfeted now, he was, at one time, one of the most prominent spokespersons of the Palestinian cause in the West and renowned as a master debater – a 'calm and careful speaker [who] used language precisely'.[9] Sayegh was also 'famous for citing, by heart, paragraphs of given UN resolutions, dates of issuance, and books with page numbers'.[10] His gift for communication is also evident in his writing, and *Zionist Colonialism in Palestine* is notable for the ease with which it translates complex historical developments into succinct, accessible language. Divided into four chapters – I) The Historical Setting of Zionist Colonialism, II) The Alliance of British Imperialism and Zionist Colonialism, III) The Character of the Zionist Settler State and IV) The Palestinians' Response: From Resistance to Liberation – the book's short length belies both its scope and importance.

When Sayegh was writing, the Palestinian cause did not enjoy the level of awareness or support it now does in progressive circles in the West, and Israel's reputation as an ostensibly 'plucky' young state in an 'unfriendly neighbourhood' had gained it widespread admiration, notably on the left. It was in this context that he approached the topic.

In the foreword, Sayegh points out the paradox that Israel was established when European colonisation had begun to retreat elsewhere. As such, the fate of Palestine was an anomaly, for at the very moment that others were beginning to enjoy their right to self-determination, the people of Palestine found 'itself helpless to prevent the culmination of a process of systematic colonisation'.[11] This process led to them losing not only *political control* over their country, but *physical occupation* of it too – 'deprived not only of its inalienable right to self-determination, but also of its elemental right to exist on its own land'.[12]

The Historical Setting of Zionist Colonialism

Sayegh skilfully analyses the formation of the Zionist movement up until the outbreak of the First World War in the book's opening chapter. He explains that, although it emerged in the context of late nineteenth century European nationalism and colonialism – and was thus heavily imbued with their ideological temper – Zionist colonisation in Palestine was distinct from European colonisation elsewhere in three crucial ways.

Firstly, unlike other European settlers,

typically animated by economic or 'politico-imperialist' motives, Zionist colonists 'were driven to the colonisation of Palestine by the desire to attain nationhood for themselves, and to establish a Jewish state'.[13]

Secondly, while other European settlers tolerated the existence of indigenous populations, whom they commonly exploited as cheap labour, Zionism's aims – both territorial and political – could not be achieved so long as the Palestinians remained on their land. Therefore, unlike other European colonialist projects of the period, it 'was essentially incompatible with the continued existence of the 'native population' in the coveted country'.[14]

Finally, other European settlers could rely on the protection of their imperial sponsors to assist them settling in their chosen territory. By contrast, not only did the Zionist movement lack such support at this stage, it was likely to encounter resistance from the Ottomans.

Sayegh assesses the programme the Zionist movement adopted to counteract these obstacles along three lines: organisation, colonisation and negotiation. In so doing, he makes it clear that unlike many of their ideological heirs in the present day, Zionists of this formative era had no qualms acknowledging the explicitly colonial nature of their venture.

Organisationally, as the movement lacked 'a state-structure in a home-base of its own to master-mind and supervise the process of overseas colonisation' it needed to build a quasi-state structure in its place.[15] The World Zionist Organisation, active to this day, was established in 1897 for that purpose. With regards to the process of colonisation itself, the haphazard, 'mixed philanthropic-colonial venture' pursued previously with limited success was replaced with a more systematic approach.[16] This entailed the establishment of several institutions from 1897 onwards, all geared towards planning, financing and facilitating the arrival of Zionist colonisers in Palestine – these included The Jewish Colonial Trust, The Colonisation Commission and The Jewish National Fund.

The third avenue, negotiation, entailed a diplomatic effort to try and foster the political conditions conducive to colonisation. This consisted primarily of an unsuccessful attempt to gain support from the Ottomans through financial and other incentives and, to a lesser extent, by making similar overtures to Germany and Britain. As summarised by Joseph Massad, 'Zionism could only be realised through a colonial-settler project, which its founders understood was achievable only through an alliance with colonial powers'.[17]

Concluding the first chapter, Sayegh makes an important point: notwithstanding its growing organisation and militancy, up to the outbreak of the First World War, the Zionist movement's success had been limited. Its appeal remained narrow – Zionists constituted a tiny percentage of the Jewish population worldwide – and colonisation had proceeded so slowly that after thirty years, Jews still accounted for under 8 percent of the total population of Palestine and were in possession of no more than 2.5 percent of its land. Furthermore, the movement had not been able to gain the patronage of the Ottomans or any other imperial power. [18]

The Alliance of British Imperialism and Zionist Colonialism

A key turning point occurred during the First World War when the Zionist movement formed an alliance of convenience with Britain. It is this development and its implications that Sayegh analyses in the book's second chapter. Britain's pre-war policy towards the Ottoman Empire had been concerned with maintaining its territorial integrity in Asia. This approach changed once the Ottomans joined the Central Powers, leading Britain, France and Tsarist Russia to draw up plans for the anticipated division of the spoils.

Subsequently, Britain's desire to keep any rival European power away from the Suez Canal – crucial for securing the sea passage to India – led it to renege on an earlier agreement that would have seen the 'internationalisation' of most of Palestine in the case of an Ottoman defeat. In its place, Britain began to lean towards the Zionist movement, realising that a 'Jewish homeland' in Palestine could provide Britain with the pretext needed to place the territory east of Suez under its control – or what Ronald Storrs, the first British governor of Jerusalem, described as 'a little loyal Jewish Ulster in a sea of potentially hostile Arabism'.[19] As Sayegh puts it in characteristically succinct fashion, '[r]eciprocal interests had thus come to bind British Imperialism and Zionist Colonialism'.[20]

It was in this context that Britain made the now infamous Balfour Declaration on 2 November 1917, proclaiming its support for the establishment of a Jewish 'national home' in Palestine. This promise was then incorporated into the text of the Palestine Mandate, awarded to Britain by the League of Nations in the aftermath of the war. Once Britain established its rule, it wasted little time in fostering the conditions needed for Zionist colonisation to flourish.

Sayegh explains how the British authorities, ignoring Palestinian opposition, opened the country up to Zionist immigration and allowed the settler community to establish what by 1937 had become a 'state within a state'.[21] Britain permitted the Zionist community to run its own schools and maintain a military force, while at the same time denying the Palestinian community analogous facilities and suppressing their attempts at self-determination. After thirty years of Mandate rule, the Zionist settler-community had grown twelve times in size since 1917 and represented almost one third of the total population of Palestine.[22] Perhaps more importantly, under Britain's auspices, it had developed what Sayegh terms 'its own quasi-government institutions and a sizable military establishment'.[23]

Britain had not entered into this partnership altruistically, so in order to justify its continued presence, whenever Zionism 'sought to accelerate the processes of state-building... Britain pulled in the opposite direction to slow them down'.[24] Sayegh details succinctly how this irresolvable tension ultimately caused the alliance to break down – violently so by the end of the Second World War. Britain's depleted condition and India's looming independence lessened its interest in maintaining its presence in Palestine, and the growing opposition of the newly-emerging independent Arab states forced Britain 'to exercise some restraint in its formerly whole-hearted support for the Zionist cause'.[25] Crucial too was the growing Arab nationalist movement from below and the protests, boycotts, general strikes and guerrilla attacks it carried out across the region.

The US, the triumphant and emerging global hegemonic power, offered Zionism the prospect of an alternative Western sponsor for what would prove a 'new fateful phase of its capture of Palestine'. Described by Sayegh as a 'willing candidate' for such a role, the US then 'led a European-American majority to overrule the opposition of an Afro-Asian minority' in the UN, and endorsed 'the establishment of a colonial Zionist state in the Afro-Asian bridge, the Arab land of Palestine'.[26]

Concluding this chapter, Sayegh explains that Israel's 'vital and continuing association' with imperialism, its introduction of Western colonialism into Palestine and its 'chosen pattern of racial exclusiveness and self-segregation renders it an alien society in the Middle East'.[27] As its founding figure,

David Ben-Gurion, himself proclaimed: 'The State of Israel is a part of the Middle East only in geography'.[28] It is the distinctive characteristics of this state that Sayegh assesses in the next chapter.

The Character of the Zionist Settler-State

> The racist regime in occupied Palestine and the racist regimes in Zimbabwe and South Africa have a common imperialist origin ... having the same racist structure and being organically linked in their policy aimed at repression of the dignity and integrity of the human being. Organisation of African Unity, Resolution on Palestine, August 1975

The three defining characteristics of the Zionist settler-state as defined by Sayegh are (1) its racial complexion and conduct; (2) its addiction to violence; and (3) its expansionist stance.[29]

As Sayegh maintains, racism 'is not an acquired trait of the Zionist settler-state. Nor is it an accidental, passing feature of the Israeli scene. It is congenital, essential and permanent ... inherent in the very ideology of Zionism'.[30] Belief in the national oneness of all Jews – based on ostensibly common ancestry, not a religious or linguistic-based identity, is a central tenet of Zionism.[31] Sayegh identifies three corollaries this explicit racial identification gives rise to: 'racial self-segregation, racial exclusiveness, and racial supremacy'.[32] It is these characteristics which made the forced removal of the indigenous population of Palestine central to the Zionist project.

Prior to the successful implementation of Plan Dalet and the resultant *Nakba* of 1948, the Zionist movement had contented itself with segregation from the Palestinians through instituting a systematic boycott of their produce and labour. Contrary to liberal-Zionist journalist Owen Jones' claim that '[t]he collective communities of the *kibbut-*

zim seemed like incubators of a new socialist society',[33] a principle was established that 'only Jewish labour would be employed in Zionist colonies'.[34] The *Histadrut* or General Organisation of Jewish Workers was established in 1920 specifically for this purpose, and as early as 1895, Theodor Herzl, the 'spiritual father' of Israel, was planning to 'spirit the penniless population [i.e. the Palestinians] across the frontier by denying it employment'.[35] Indeed, organisations such as the Jewish National Fund 'vigilantly ensured the observation of that fundamental principle'.[36]

Sayegh, further demonstrating the racial exclusiveness inherent to the Zionist project, highlights the treatment that Palestinians who Zionist forces were unable to dislodge in 1948 have received since. He argues that through the systematic oppression of this internal population, Israel 'has learned all the lessons which the various discriminatory regimes of white settler-states in Asia and Africa can teach it'. Sayegh outlines the manifold official and unofficial oppressive measures these Palestinians faced – measures that have only grown more onerous and engrained since then – and remarks that, whereas 'the Afrikaner apostles of *apartheid* ... brazenly proclaim their sin, the Zionist practitioners of *apartheid* in Palestine beguilingly protest their innocence'.[37]

Events since the publication of Sayegh's book offer grim confirmation of his assertion that Israel is addicted to violence. Since 1965, it has perpetuated an unbroken line of violent acts against the Palestinians too long to list here – both in and outside of Mandate territory. Echoing Sayegh's analysis, after Israeli snipers had massacred Palestinian protestors on the Gaza border in May 2018, Saree Makdisi commented, '[i]t is not possible for a settler-colonial regime to racially enable one people at the expense of another people without the use of violence'.[38]

Furthermore, the target of this violence

has not only been the Palestinians, Israel has also committed multiple aggressions against neighbouring states, including Lebanon, Syria and Egypt. It forcibly depopulated the Golan Heights in Syria and has illegally occupied this region since 1967. Israel has also played an integral role in the ongoing war against Syria, repeatedly launching airstrikes against it in recent years. This trend underlines Sayegh's prescient observation that Israel is perpetually expansionist in nature, for not only has it consistently expanded the territory under its control, it has refused to ever declare its borders.

The fate that befell the PRC itself – subjected to multiple acts of violence by Israeli forces during its expansionist war against Lebanon in 1982 – offers particularly direct evidence of Sayegh's tragically accurate foresight. As he wrote, expansion to the borders of so-called *Eretz Israel* 'is the 'unfinished business' of Zionism. It cannot fail to be the main preoccupation of the Zionist movement, and of the Zionist state, in the future'.[39]

The Palestinians' Response: From Resistance to Liberation

In the book's final chapter, Sayegh analyses the Palestinians' responses to Zionist colonisation. He divides this into five stages, beginning with the Palestinians' initially welcoming attitude to the early Jewish settlers,[40] moving through the various phases and avenues of resistance the Palestinian community put up against both the British authorities and Zionist forces up to 1964 with the formation of the PLO. In spite of this resistance, that reached its pinnacle in the Great Palestinian Revolt from 1936 until 1939, the bulk of the Palestinian population was forcibly dispossessed in 1948 – their 'unyielding resistance and their costly sacrifices had failed to avert national catastrophe'.[41]

Sayegh stresses that these sacrifices were not made in vain, however, for '[r]ights un-

defended are rights surrendered. Unopposed and acquiesced in, usurpation is legitimised by default'.[42] The Palestinians' unyielding resistance and affirmation of their rights and heritage therefore ensured that Israel has 'remained a usurper, lacking even the semblance of legitimacy'.[43]

Though he stresses that liberation must be spearheaded by the Palestinians themselves, Sayegh contends that the 'problem of Palestine… is not the concern of Palestinians alone'. Israel's commitment to expansion is also a threat to the security and territorial integrity of the Arab states. Furthermore, as a colonial venture, 'which anomalously came to bloom precisely when colonialism was beginning to fade away, it is in fact a challenge to all anti-colonial peoples… For, in the final analysis', Sayegh writes, 'the cause of anti-colonialism and liberation is one and indivisible'.[44]

He concludes that as a system 'animated by doctrines of racial self-segregation, racial exclusiveness, and racial supremacy' – that then translates those doctrines into 'ruthless practices of racial discrimination and oppression' – the political systems erected by Zionist colonialism in Palestine must be recognised as a menace to all those 'dedicated to the safeguarding and enhancement of the dignity of man. For whenever and wherever the dignity of but one single human being is violated, in pursuance of the creed of racism, a heinous sin is committed against the dignity of all men, everywhere'.[45]

At a time when solidarity with the Palestinians is increasingly under attack, slandered as anti-Semitic or even criminalised, Sayegh's words serve as a timely reminder of why such solidarity has never been more important to express.

Editor's note - originally published March 2021 on Liberated Texts

References

1   Daniel Patrick Moynihan, 'Response to United Nations Resolution 3379', 1975.

2   *The New York Times* reported that 'United States embassies around the world were instructed to put maximum pressure to secure the repeal'. It went on to state that the vote 'reflected the shifting political currents of recent years, the Persian Gulf war in particular, which split the Arab and Islamic worlds, and the changes in the former Soviet bloc, fostered by the collapse of Communism'. 'U.N. Repeals Its '75 Resolution Equating Zionism With Racism', *New York Times*, 1991.

3   'Palestine Liberation' Literature, *Patterns of Prejudice*, 1:6, (1967).

4   Clayborne Carson, *In Struggle: SNCC and the Black Awakening of the 1960s* (Harvard University Press, 1981), 266-269.

5   Ihsan A. Hijazi, 'Israelis Looted Archives of P.L.O Officials Say', *The New York Times*, 1982.

6   Responsibility for the bombing was claimed by a group called the Front for the Liberation of Lebanon from Foreigners (FLLF) which was later revealed to be 'a creation of Israel, a fictitious group used by senior officials to hide their country's hand in a deadly "terrorist" campaign'. Remi Brulin, 'How the Israeli military censor killed a story about "terrorist" bombing campaign in Lebanon in 1980s', *Mondoweiss*, 2019.

7   Munir Fasheh, 'Graham-Brown, Education, Repression and Liberation', *Middle East Report*, 136/137 (October-December 1985).

8   On this topic, see Steven Salaita, *Israel's Dead Soul* (Temple University Press, 2011).

9   As'ad Abukhalil, 'Before Edward Said: a tribute to Fayez Sayegh', *Al Akhbar English*, 2014.

10   Anis F. Kassim (ed.), *The Palestine Yearbook of International Law, 1998-1999* (Brill/Nijhoff, 2000).

11   Fayez Sayegh, *Zionist Colonialism in Palestine* (Palestine Research Center, 1965), V.

12   Sayegh, *Zionist Colonialism*, VI.

13   Sayegh, *Zionist Colonialism*, 4-5.

14   Sayegh, *Zionist Colonialism*, 4-5.

15   Sayegh, *Zionist Colonialism*, 6.

16   Sayegh, *Zionist Colonialism*, 2.

17   Joseph Massad, 'Zionism, Anti-Semitism and Colonialism', *al Jazeera*, 2012.

18   Sayegh, *Zionist Colonialism*, 8.

19   Conn Hallinan, 'Divide and Rule', *Irish Democrat*, 2004.

20   Sayegh, *Zionist Colonialism*, 12.

21   Sayegh, *Zionist Colonialism*, 14 (quoting Britain's Palestine Royal Commission, 1937).

22   Sayegh, *Zionist Colonialism*, 15.

23   Sayegh, *Zionist Colonialism*, 15.

24   Sayegh, *Zionist Colonialism*, 15.

25   Sayegh, *Zionist Colonialism*, 15.

26   Sayegh, *Zionist Colonialism*, 16. Two years after the release of Sayegh's book, and in language seemingly informed by it, the Afro-Asian Writers' Association condemned Israel as 'an imperialist base and… tool used for aggressive purposes against Arab states in order to delay their progress… and as a bridge-head which neo-colonialism relies on in order to maintain its influence over African and Asian states'. Resolution on Palestine of the Third Afro-Asian Writers' Conference (March 25-30, 1967, Beirut, Lebanon).

27   Sayegh, *Zionist Colonialism*, 19.

28   David Ben-Gurion, *Rebirth and Destiny of Israel* (Philosophical Library, 1954), 489.

29   Sayegh, *Zionist Colonialism*, 21.

30   Sayegh, *Zionist Colonialism*, 21.

31   As Sayegh notes, at this time relatively few Zionists were 'believing or practising Jews' and Hebrew 'was resuscitated only after the birth of Zionism', Sayegh, *Zionist Colonialism*, 21.

32   Sayegh, *Zionist Colonialism*, 21.

33   As quoted in Oliver Eagleton, 'Vicious, Horrible People', *New Left Review*, 127 (Jan/Feb 2021).

34   Sayegh, *Zionist Colonialism*, 25.

35   Sayegh, *Zionist Colonialism*, 26.

36   Sayegh, *Zionist Colonialism*, 25.

37   Sayegh, *Zionist Colonialism*, 27.

38   Saree Makdisi, 'Kill and Kill and Kill', *Counterpunch*, 2018.

39   Sayegh, *Zionist Colonialism*, 38.

40   Sayegh notes that even Herzl himself commented on the 'friendly attitude of the population', Sayegh, *Zionist Colonialism*, 39.

41   Sayegh, *Zionist Colonialism*, 46.

42   Sayegh, *Zionist Colonialism*, 46.

43   Sayegh, *Zionist Colonialism*, 46.

44   Sayegh, *Zionist Colonialism*, 46.

45   Sayegh, *Zionist Colonialism*, 46.

The city night is dark apart from the glow of missiles,
silent apart from the sound of bombing,
terrifying apart from the reassurance of prayer,
black except for the light of the martyrs,
Good night, Gaza.

The final tweet of Heba Abu Nada, written on October 8th 2023.[1]

Abu Nada was a published poet, novelist and educator. She was killed by an Israeli airstrike on October 20th 2023. She was 32 years old.

References

1   Translated from the original Arabic by Louis Allday.

Anti-Zionism as Decolonisation

Leila Shomali & Lara Kilani

As horrifying scenes from Gaza have been recorded, published, and replayed around the world, people have been jolted into action and have thrown themselves into solidarity work. This surge of activism is fuelled by visceral reactions to the harrowing realities of Israel's ongoing genocide unfolding on the global stage. People are realising, by the thousands, that zionism is a political program of indigenous erasure and primitive resource accumulation.

Many new activists and reactivated organisers seek to translate their emotional responses into tangible support. They are also searching for community hubs, often in the form of organisations, that confront zionism and colonialism – the root cause of this genocide. Whether activists know it or not, they are looking for an anti-zionist home for their organising efforts. It is exactly the moment, therefore, to provide an honest discussion on some of the essential characteristics of this organising, firmly rooted in the principles of Palestinian liberation and decolonisation, peeling away any remaining layers of confusion or mystery.

If we accept, as those with even the most rudimentary understanding of history do, that zionism is an ongoing process of settler-colonialism, then the undoing of zion-ism requires anti-zionism, which should be understood as a process of decolonisation. Anti-zionism as a decolonial ideology then becomes rightly situated as an indigenous liberation movement. The resulting implication is two-fold. First, decolonial organising requires that we extract ourselves from the limitations of existing structures of power and knowledge and imagine a new, just world. Second, this understanding clarifies that the caretakers of anti-zionist thought are indigenous communities resisting colonial erasure, and it is from this analysis that the strategies, modes, and goals of decolonial praxis should flow. In simpler terms: Palestinians committed to decolonisation, not Western-based NGOs, are the primary authors of anti-zionist thought. We write this as a Palestinian and a Palestinian-American who live and work in Palestine, and have seen the impact of so-called 'Western values' and how the centring of the 'human rights' paradigm disrupts real decolonial efforts in Palestine and abroad. This is carried out in favour of maintaining the status quo and gaining proximity to power, using our slogans emptied of Palestinian historical analysis.

Anti-zionist organising is not a new notion, but until now the use of the term in organising circles has been mired with misunderstandings, vague definitions, or minimised outright. Some have incorrectly described anti-zionism as amounting to activities or thought limited to critiques of the present Israeli government[1] – this is a dangerous misrepresentation. Understanding anti-zionism as decolonisation requires the articulation of a political movement with material, articulated goals: the restitution of ancestral territories and upholding the inviolable principle of indigenous repatriation and through the right of return, coupled with the deconstruction of zionist structures and the reconstitution of governing frameworks that are conceived, directed, and implemented by Palestinians.

Anti-zionism illuminates the necessity to return power to the indigenous community and the need for frameworks of justice and accountability for the settler communities that have waged a bloody, unrelenting hundred-year war on the people of Palestine. It means that anti-zionism is much more than a slogan.

A liberation movement

Given the implications of defining anti-zionism, we must reorient ourselves around it within the framework of a liberation movement. This emphasises the strategic importance of control over the narrative and principles of anti-zionism in the context of global decolonial efforts. As Steven Salaita points out in 'Hamas is a Figment of Your Imagination', zionism and liberal zionism continue to influence the shape of Palestinian resistance:

> Zionists [have] a type of rhetorical control in the public sphere: they get to determine the culture of the native; they get to prescribe (and proscribe) the contours of resistance; they get to adjudicate the work of national liberation. Palestinians are entrapped by the crude and self-serving imagination of the oppressor.[2]

We have to wrestle back our right to narration, and can use anti-zionist thought as a guide for liberation. We must reclaim anti-zionist praxis from those who would only use it as a headline in a fundraising email.

While our collective imaginations have not fully articulated what a liberated and decolonised Palestine looks like, the rough contours have been laid out repeatedly. Ask any Palestinian refugee displaced from Haifa, the lands of Sheikh Muwannis, or Deir Yassin – they will tell that a decolonised Palestine is, at a minimum, the right of Palestinians' return to an autonomous political unit from the river to the sea.

When self-proclaimed 'anti-zionists' use rhetoric like 'Israel-Palestine' – or worse, 'Palestine-Israel' – we wonder: where do you think 'Israel' exists? On which land does it lay, if not Palestine? This is nothing more than an attempt to legitimise a colonial state; the name you are looking for is Palestine – no hyphen required. At a minimum, anti-zionist formations should cut out language that forces upon Palestinians and non-Palestinian allies the violence of colonial theft.

The settler/native relationship

Understanding the settler/native relationship is essential in anti-zionist organising. It means confronting the 'settler' designation in zionist settler-colonialism – a class status indicating one's place in the larger settler-colonial systems of power. Anti-zionist discourse should critically challenge the zionist (re)framing of history through colonial instruments, such as the Oslo Accords and an over-reliance on international law frameworks, through which they differentiate Israeli settlers in Tel Aviv and those in West Bank settlements.

Suggesting that some Israeli cities are settlements while others are not perpetuates zionist framing, granting legitimacy to colonial control according to arbitrary geographical divisions in Palestine, and further dividing the land into disparate zones. Anti-zionist analysis understands that 'settlers' are not only residents of 'illegal' West Bank settlements like Kiryat Arba and Efrat, but also those in Safad and Petah Tikvah. Ask any Palestinian who is living in exile from Haifa; they will tell you the Israelis living in their homes are also settlers.

The common choice to centre the Oslo Accords, international humanitarian law, and the human rights paradigm over socio-historical Palestinian realities not only limits our analysis and political interventions; it restricts our imagination regarding what kind of future Palestinians deserve, sidelining questions of decolonisation to convince us that it is the *new, bad* settlers in the West Bank who are the source of violence. *Legitimate* settlers, who reside within the bounds of Palestinian geographies stolen in 1948 like Tel Aviv and West Jerusalem, are different within this narrative. Like Breaking the Silence, they can supposedly be enlightened by learning the error of colonial violence carried out in service of the *bad* settlers. They can even be our solidarity partners – all without having to sacrifice a crumb of colonial privilege or denounce pre-1967 zionist violence in any of its cruel manifestations.

As a result of this course of thought, solidarity organisations often showcase particular Israelis – those who renounce state violence in service of the *bad* settlers and their ongoing colonisation of the West Bank – in roles as professionals and peacemakers, positioning them on an equal intellectual, moral, or class footing with Palestinians. There is no recognition of the inherent imbalance of power between these Israelis and the Palestinians they purport to be in solidarity with – stripping away their settler status. The settler is taken out of the historical-political context which afforded them privileged status on stolen land, and is given the power to delineate the Palestinian experience. This is part of the historical occlusion of the zionist narrative, overlooking the context of settler-colonialism to read the settler as an individual, and omitting their class status as a settler.

Misreading 'decolonisation'

It is essential to note that Palestinians have

never rejected Jewish indigeneity in Palestine. However, the liberation movement has differentiated between zionist settlers and Jewish natives. Palestinians have established a clear and rational framework for this distinction, like in the Thawabet, the National Charter of Palestine from 1968. Article 6 states, 'The Jews who had normally resided in Palestine until the beginning of the Zionist invasion will be considered Palestinians.'[3]

When individuals misread 'decolonisation' as 'the mass killing or expulsion of Jews,' it is often a reflection of their own entanglement in colonialism or a result of zionist propaganda. Perpetuating this rhetoric is a deliberate misinterpretation of Palestinian thought, which has maintained this position over a century of indigenous organising.

Even after 100 years of enduring ethnic cleansing, whole communities bombed and entire family lines erased, Palestinians have never, as a collective, called for the mass killing of Jews or Israelis. Anti-zionism cannot shy away from employing the historical-political definitions of 'settler' and 'indigenous' in their discourse to confront ahistorical readings of Palestinian decolonial thought and zionist propaganda.

The zionist version of 'all lives matter'

As we see, settler-colonialism secures the position of the settler, imbuing them with rights, in this case, a divine right of conquest. As such, zionism ensures that settlers' rights supersede those of indigenous people at the latter's expense. Knowing this, the liberal slogan 'equal rights for all people' requires deeper consideration. Rather than placing the emphasis on the deconstruction of the settler state and the violence inherent to it, which eternally serve the settler at the direct detriment of indigenous communities, the slogan suggests that Palestinians simply need to secure more rights within the violent system. But 'equal rights', in the sense that those chanting this phrase mean them, will not come from attempts to rehabilitate a settler state. They can only be ensured through the decolonisation of Palestine, through the material restitution of land and resources. Without further discussion, the slogan simply serves as another mechanism of zionism, one that maintains the rights of the settler rather than emphasising the need to *restore* rights to indigenous communities, who have long been the victims of settlers' rights.

Anti-zionists cannot both denounce settler-colonialism and zionism, and centre advocacy on the claim that settlers should have equal, immutable rights. zionists would have you believe that their state has always existed, that Israelis have always lived on the land. But a brief reference to recent history reminds us that anti-zionism must confront the ongoing mechanisms materially advancing the development of colonies in Palestine.

In 2022 alone, zionist institutions invested almost $100 million, transferring some 60,000 new settlers from Russia, Eastern Europe, the United States, and France to help secure a demographic majority and ensure a physical presence on indigenous lands.[4] This only happens by maintaining the forced displacement of Palestinians, and by violently displacing them anew as we see on a daily basis, particularly across the rural West Bank.

There is no moral legitimacy in the suggestion that these settlers have a 'right' to live on stolen Palestinian land, the theft maintained by force, as long as there has been no restoration of Palestinians' rights. No theories of justice exist in mainstream ethical or philosophical discourse that advocate for a person who has stolen something to rightfully keep what they have taken. The act of theft, by definition, violates the basic principles of theories of justice, which emphasise fairness, equitable distribution of resources, and respect for individual rights and property.

Reminding people that decolonisation is not a metaphor, some activists with Israeli citizenship, including Nadav Gazit[5] and Yuula Benivolsky,[6] have taken the initiative to tangibly support Palestinian liberation and renounced their claim to settler citizenship.

When liberal NGOs champion 'equal rights for all people' with no further discussion of what this means, it is the zionist version of 'all lives matter', perpetuating – or at best, failing to question – the maintenance of systems of violence against Palestinians.

Having laid out some of the foundational concepts and definitions pertaining to zionism and anti-zionism, we can explore some essential strategies and tactics of anti-zionist organising.

Structural changes to support liberation

As anti-zionism necessitates the systematic dismantling of zionist structures, this process may include educational programs and protests, which serve as foundational activities. However, it is essential to be cautious of organising spaces and activities that become comfort zones for activists, lacking the necessary risk and failing to meaningfully challenge existing structures of zionist violence. Anti-zionist organising must involve strategic policy and legal reform that support decolonisation from afar, such as targeting laws that enable international charities to fund Israeli settler militias and settlement expansion.[7] After all, our aim from abroad should be to make structural changes to advance decolonisation, not simply shift public sentiment about Palestine.

Decolonial approaches abroad include changing the internal structures of institutions that support colonisation: charities, churches, synagogues, social clubs, and other donor institutions. This includes entities that many international activists are personally, professionally, and financially linked to, such as the nonprofits we coordinate with and large grant-making institutions like the Open Society Foundation and Carnegie Corporation of New York.

An organisation's commitment to solidarity and conceptualisation of resistance should be transparent. Its ideals should be clear to potential newcomers as well as its donors. We have seen, too many times, organisations intentionally obfuscate what they stand for so they relate to a broad mass of people while at the same time being palatable to liberal donors. They use vague language about the future they envision, describing 'equality, justice, and a thriving future for all Palestinians and Israelis' without a thoughtful discussion of what Palestinians will need to reach this prosperity. The dual discourse phenomenon, where contradictory messages are conveyed to grassroots supporters and financial donors, is a manipulative tactic for institutional or personal gain. It should be clear from the onset that a group's efforts have one ultimate goal: from the river to the sea, Palestine will be free.

In the context of the United States, the most threatening zionist institutions are the entrenched political parties which function to maintain the status quo of the American empire, not Hillel groups on university campuses or even Christian zionist churches. While the Anti-Defamation League (ADL) and the American Israel Public Affairs Committee (AIPAC) engage in forms of violence that suppress Palestinian liberation and must not be minimised, it is crucial to recognise that the most consequential institutions in the context of settler-colonialism are not exclusively Jewish in their orientation or representation: the Republican and Democratic Party in the United States do arguably more to manufacture public consent for the slaughtering of Palestinians than the ADL and AIPAC combined. Even the Progressive Caucus and the majority of 'The Squad' are guilty of this.

These internal challenges to the institutions and communities we belong to are, by definition, risky and sacrificial – but essential and liberatory. They require confrontation, and likely the withholding of support and material resources, in order to usher in change. As we have seen over the last months, merely organising protests to pressure politicians without the explicit intent to withdraw electoral and financial support from political parties and institutions is fundamentally flawed.[8] It also does not secure the desired result: on November 28, 2023, in the midst of Israel's genocide of the Palestinians in Gaza, members of the US House of Representatives voted 421 to 1 (with the 1 unaligned to any decolonisation movement) to support a bill that equates anti-zionism to antisemitism.[9] Members of 'The Squad' who did not vote for the bill did not vote against it, either.

Politicians, organisational leaders, and funding institutions must see the real political consequences of their decisions to support genocide. Reluctance within the executive leadership of international solidarity organisations to hold elected officials accountable is a red flag, as we cannot balance our loyalties between liberation and temporary political convenience. Anti-zionism requires more than political organising that is targeted at those intentionally maintaining white supremacy through zionism; it requires that we wager our access to power to dismantle mechanisms of oppression. We must stop betting on the longevity of zionism.

When we properly decouple zionism from Judaism and understand it as a process of indigenous erasure and primitive resource accumulation, the dominant political formations, the armaments industry, and the high-tech security sector are easily understood as indispensable institutions in the broader zionist project. These bodies also materially benefit from the status quo of zionist colonisation, and therefore wield their power to maintain it. This is part of a larger function of these formations to uphold white supremacy, imperialism, and colonialism globally – systems that harm *all* communities, albeit unequally. This helps us recognise that zionism does not serve to benefit Jewish people, even if this is not the primary reason we should abolish it. Equating global Jewish communities' safety and prosperity with the safeguarding of colonial violence is an antisemitic and fallacious argument. It contends that in order to thrive, Jewish communities must displace, dominate, incarcerate, oppress, and murder Palestinians.

This relates to the earlier discussion of understanding Palestinians as the authors and caretakers of anti-zionist decolonial thought. We must be cautious not to portray anti-zionism as belonging in any exclusive way to Jewish activists, or requiring Jewish organisations' initiative. Characterising anti-zionism as a practice necessarily spearheaded by Jewish activists, rather than acknowledging it as a decolonial praxis aimed at deconstructing the institutions maintaining the colonisation of Palestine displaces Palestinian decolonial leadership. By placing undue emphasis on the role of Jewish organisations, we de-centre Palestinian knowledge, experience, and decolonial efforts in favour of non-Palestinian agencies. This is a grave error. Such a conflation not only misrepresents the objectives of anti-zionism but also inadvertently contributes to the continuation of antisemitic sentiments by equating Judaism and colonialism.

Bold solidarity

In summary, anti-zionism is not a slogan, but a process of decolonisation and liberation. Palestinians committed to resisting zionism and erasure are the caretakers of this political movement. Cities such as Tel Aviv and Modi'in are settlements, just like Itamar or Tel Rumeida in the West Bank. Decolonisation does not imply the displacement of all Jewish communities in Palestine; however, it is crucial to recognise that not every individual identifying as Jewish is indigenous to Palestine. This basic framework must be unabashedly articulated by anti-zionist organisations and allies in their advocacy. Anti-zionist organising should move towards dismantling the colonial structures through the changing of laws and policies of the institutions and formations most essential to the Israeli state project.

This essay is not an exhaustive manual; instead, it begins a much-needed conversation and presents central principles of anti-zionist praxis. These principles are non-negotiable and represent some of the markers of anti-zionist organising. These anti-zionist indicators should not be sprinkled about through emails or social media posts that one has to dig for, but should be glaringly evident in our work and analysis.

Anti-zionism and solidarity should be bold. Palestinians deserve nothing less.

Leila Shomali is a Palestinian PhD candidate in International Law at Maynooth University Ireland and a member of the Good Shepherd Collective.

Lara Kilani is a Palestinian-American researcher, PhD student, and member of the Good Shepherd Collective.

Acknowledgements: We would like to thank Em Cohen and Omar Zahzah for their meticulous editing and thoughtful suggestions.

References

1   'Our Approach to Zionism', *Jewish Voice for Peace*, 2023.
2   Steve Salaita, 'Hamas is a Figment of Your Imagination', *stevesalaita.com*, 2023.
3   'The Palestinian National Charter: Resolutions of the Palestine National Council' July 1-17, 1968.
4   Zvika Klein, 'Aliyah up 128% this year, with 60,000 new immigrants in past Jewish year', *The Jerusalem Post*, 2022.
5   Nadav Gazit, 'Why I am renouncing my Israeli citizenship', *Prism*, 2023.
6   'Woman renounces her Israeli citizenship due to Gaza tragedy', *TRT World*, 2023.
7   'Israel: racist settler group misusing charitable funds to displace Palestinians', *MEMO*, 2023.
8   Lara Kilani and Leila Shomali, 'To "push them left" we will need more than protests', *Mondoweiss*, 2023.
9   Congress.gov. "Congressional Record." December 9, 2023. https://www.congress.gov/congressional-record/volume-169/issue-195/daily-digest/article/D1224-1.

Printed in the USA
CPSIA information can be obtained
at www.ICGtesting.com
LVHW060253300124
770082LV00030B/471